With New Testament eyes

With New Testament eyes

Pictures of Christ in the Old Testament

Genesis to Job

Henry T. Mahan

 Evangelical Press

EVANGELICAL PRESS
12 Wooler Street, Darlington, Co. Durham, DL1 1RQ, England

© Evangelical Press 1993
First published 1993

British Library cataloguing in Publication Data available

ISBN 0 85234 304 3

Scripture quotations in this publication are from the Authorized (King James) Version.

Printed and bound in Great Britain at the Bath Press, Avon.

Contents

1. The Fall

Genesis 3:1-21

Chapters 1 and 2 of Genesis give an account of how God brought the world into being and created man in his own image (Gen. 1:26-29; Eccles. 7:29). God gave to Adam the law concerning the tree of the knowledge of good and evil (Gen. 2:15-17). How long Adam remained obedient we do not know, but chapter 3 gives an account of his disobedience and fall.

v. 1. Little is known about the serpent whom Satan used to tempt Eve. Some say that he was more naked, as they were, having no hair as the other animals. Some say that he was more beautiful, wise and cunning (Matt. 10:16; 2 Cor. 11:3). Some ask the question: 'Why would Eve stand and talk with an animal?' While there are many questions we cannot answer, several things are quite clear.

1. Satan (Lucifer, the devil) was a great angel with power, majesty and glory before he fell (Isa. 14:15; Luke 10:17-18), and it was Satan who appeared and talked to Eve in this particular form called 'the serpent'. He was behind the entire temptation.
2. Eve was evidently alone; no mention is made of Adam at this time. In all probability she was near the tree, or even looking at it.
3. Satan's question to Eve may have suggested the following: 'You are superior creatures; the whole earth is supposed to be in subjection to you; yet you are not totally free nor fully blessed, for there is something God is withholding from you and will not allow you to have. **Hath God said, Ye shall *not* eat of every tree of the garden?'**

vv. 2-3. Eve replied, 'We may eat of the trees in the garden, but not of the tree of the knowledge of good and evil.' She knew the commandment and repeated it to Satan, although she added, **'Neither shall ye touch it'** (Gen. 1:29-30; 2:16-17).

v. 4. **'Ye shall not surely die.'** This is a direct denial of the Word of God. This is today, and always has been, Satan's way — to deny the Word of God.

v. 5.

1. 'This is merely a threat from God to keep you in subjection to him. He will not carry it out.'

2. 'God knows all things, and he knows that if you eat of this tree, the eyes of your understanding will be opened, and you will know things that you do not know now.'

3. 'You will be like God, or you will be gods yourselves and know good and evil. You will be greater and wiser, under no control from God.' He may have eaten of the fruit himself to demonstrate to the woman that she would not die, for he did not die nor change upon eating it.

v. 6. Eve, being deceived by the serpent (1 Tim. 2:13-14), was convinced that the tree was good for the *flesh*, pleasant to the *eyes*, and a fruit that would make one *wise* (1 John 2:15-16). She ate it. Probably nothing happened; for it was upon Adam's eating the fruit that the fate of man depended, not the action of the woman; for Adam was the federal head, the representative of all our race (Rom. 5:12,17-19; 1 Cor. 15:21-22,45-48). She gave the fruit to Adam, and he ate of it willingly and knowingly.

v. 7.

1. 'Their eyes were opened' — not to advanced knowledge, nor to things pleasant and profitable, but to things distressing — evil. They saw they had been deceived and had lost communion with God.

2. They knew they were naked, and they felt things they had never known before, such as shame, guilt, fear and hate. The robe of purity and innocence had been stripped from their souls and they were ashamed and afraid.

3. They began to try to cover themselves with leaves. The death and damage were inward; outwardly they were unchanged as yet, but they were dead *spiritually* (Matt. 15:17-20; Ps. 58:3; Jer. 17:9). They fell out of God and purity into themselves, from partakers of the divine nature to a nature of evil and flesh only (John 3:5-6). Adam's apron of leaves could not cover his true shame and guilt, nor restore him to God's favour. His fallen nature produced guilt (v. 8), fear and shame (v. 10), self-righteousness and hatred (v. 12).

v. 15. Here is the first promise in the Scriptures of our Redeemer, the Lord Jesus Christ — the seed of woman! All born into this world are the seed of men except Christ, who is born of the virgin (Isa. 7:14; 9:6; Luke 1:28-35).

Christ, the woman's seed, the God-man, bone of our bone and flesh of our flesh, will come into the world and by his life and death destroy Satan and all evil and death on behalf of his people. Satan will bruise his *heel;* his human life will suffer and die. But he will bruise Satan's *head,* which is his power, government and reign (Heb. 2:14-18).

v. 21. Another picture and type of Christ is given here. God slew an animal, shed its blood and made coats of skin for the guilty sinners. The first blood ever shed on earth was shed in sacrifice to cover a man's sin. Christ, the Lamb of God, must shed his blood and die to put away our sins and provide a robe of righteousness for us (2 Cor. 5:21). Since God is infinitely and unchangeably holy, sin can never be passed over without full payment and satisfaction of the justice of God (Exod. 34:7; Josh. 24:19).

Questions
1. What did Paul mean when he wrote, 'In Adam all die'? (1 Cor. 15:22).
2. In what ways do people still try to 'cover themselves' before God?
3. What may we learn of Christ's substitutionary work from this passage?

2. Abel's offering

Genesis 4:1-15

v. 1. We have been bound in our thinking by pictures and stories in children's Bible story-books that present a totally unrealistic view of the first family. Adam and Eve are pictured with only two sons, one of whom killed the other and left them with only Cain, the fugitive, until Seth was born when Adam was 130 years old, There were no children born to Adam and Eve *before* the Fall, but we can be certain that there were many born to them *after* the Fall (Gen. 5:4). Cain was the first man-child. It is not certain that he was the first child, or that Abel was the second. One commentary suggests that by the time Seth was born, Adam probably had as many as 32,000 descendants. As we can see in reading the Scriptures, the birth of a female was not usually even mentioned — only the male, and not all of them by any means. It is believed that when Cain was born to Eve, she thought he was the promised Messiah: **'I have gotten *the* man from the Lord.'**

v. 2. God has singled out these sons of Adam to teach to all redemption by blood (Lev. 17:11; Heb. 9:22) and to condemn salvation by works (1 Peter 1:18-20). The way of Abel is the way of grace, and the way of Cain is the way of works. Here is the crossroads, and all who attempt to come to God must choose one or the other. There are only two religions in the world — grace and works (Rom. 11:6). Cain was a farmer and Abel was a shepherd.

v. 3. Cain and Abel were not young boys at this time, but they were evidently heads of households with wives and children and occupations. Nor were these the first sacrifices offered to God for sin, for it is certain that God had instructed Adam as to how he was to worship and approach the living God. Adam, in turn, had taught his sons and daughters, as Abraham would later teach Isaac (Gen. 22:6-7). As their father had done before them, Cain and Abel, as heads of families, brought their sacrifices and offerings to God. Cain brought the fruit of the ground, which he had raised, and Abel brought a lamb.

vv. 4-5.

What was wrong with Cain's sacrifice?

1. It was a bloodless sacrifice, thereby denying his need of the Redeemer, the Lord Jesus Christ. Cain would be his own priest, his own mediator and his own intercessor.
2. It denied that he was a sinner before God, who deserved condemnation and death. He approached God on the grounds of his own merit and works. He was proud of the fruit of his fields (Rom. 6:23).
3. He refused God's revealed way of worship and acceptance (Luke 24:44-47; Eph. 1:6-7).

Why did God have respect to Abel's offering?

1. It was an offering of faith (Heb. 11:4). Like Abraham, Abel believed God. He came to God as he was told to come.
2. It was an offering typifying Christ — the Lamb of God — as we see in the Passover lamb (Exod. 12:5-6): a *lamb,* the innocent dying for the guilty; a *male* of the first year, in the prime of life; *without spot or blemish:* Christ was without sin. They were to slay it, shed its blood and roast it with fire; Christ suffered and shed his blood for our sins.
3. It was an offering confessing his sins and owning that they deserved death. Our sins deserve the wrath of God, and in order to justify us, the Lord Jesus must die before the justice of God (Rom. 3:23-26). Christ, our substitute, made full satisfaction before the law of God and the justice of God, thereby enabling God to be just and the justifier of those who believe in Christ.

vv. 6-8.   Cain was angry and became depressed. The religion of works yields no comfort and no communion with God. Men go about their ceremonies but find no peace; they make professions and perform religious acts but find no rest nor assurance because God is not reconciled (2 Cor. 5:19).

Cain was not angry with himself, as he should have been, but he was angry with God and with his brother who believed God. Instead of looking into his own heart and finding the reason for his troubles, he turned on Abel.

Rather than repenting and coming to God by faith in Christ Jesus, Cain rose up against his brother and killed him. The first human blood shed on earth was over salvation by grace or salvation by works. Cain would come to God, not by grace through faith in Christ, but by his own works and merit (Eph. 2:8-9). This battle still rages and the results are the same. God is the same, sin is the same, men are the same, the way of life through the blood of Christ is the same, and 'the way of Cain' still persecutes the way of faith.

Questions
1. What is the difference between grace religion and works religion?
2. Why does the religion of works provide no real comfort to man?
3. Why does grace provide peace and communion with God?

3. The ark of Noah

Genesis 6, 7

In the first chapter of Genesis, God looked over the whole creation and saw that it was good (Gen. 1:31). In this sixth chapter God looked over creation and pronounced it evil (Gen. 6:5). God's elect line of promise through Seth had already been contaminated through the intermarriage of the descendants of Seth (the sons of God) with unbelievers (the daughters of men) (6:2). God in justice planned to destroy all mankind from the face of the earth (Gen. 6:7). But Noah found grace in the eyes of the Lord (Gen. 6:8). Though he would destroy all men (and justly so, for their evil), God made a covenant to preserve Noah and his family. Noah was not saved because of goodness and merit found in himself, but God was gracious to him in Christ. The judgement of the world was an act of God's wrath upon sin, and the salvation of Noah was an act of God's mercy through Christ. Verse 9 says that Noah was a just man, upright and walked with God, but his character was a *result* of the grace of God *in* him, and not the *cause* of the grace of God *to* him (1 Cor. 15:10; Eph. 2:8-10). God was pleased to show mercy to Noah and pass by all the others (Rom. 9:11-16).

As Noah prepared the ark, he preached to his generation (1 Peter 3:18-22). They refused to hear, to repent, or to enter the ark. Yet Noah believed God and when the ark was completed (before one drop of water fell), he willingly entered the ark (Gen. 7:1,5). There is a decree of God and an everlasting covenant of mercy in Christ ordaining the salvation of a number which no man can number. Christ calls them his 'sheep', given to him by the Father. They are redeemed by him and called to him by his Spirit; yet, like Noah, they hear, believe and willingly come to Christ, their ark of safety. By faith they enter into Christ. The rest of Adam's race, though warned, though preached to, and though commanded to repent and believe, will not enter (John 10:24-30).

The flood is not fiction; it is fact. The ark is not a myth; it is a fact. And as the means of deliverance from the judgement of God against sin for this man who found grace in the eyes of the Lord, the ark is a beautiful picture of our Lord Jesus Christ, by whom we are delivered from God's eternal wrath against sin (John 3:35-36).

1. The ark was the only way of deliverance

The whole world drowned; only those in the ark were saved. The water stood high above the mountains (Gen. 7:17-21), so that no house, tree, building, or mountain could serve as a refuge — only the ark.

Christ is the only Saviour (John 14:6; Acts 4:10-12; Isa. 53:4-6). This is the theme of the whole Scriptures, that Christ is *the* Redeemer, the *only* Redeemer and the *sufficient* Redeemer (1 John 5:10-13).

2. The ark was big enough for all who came

There was enough room for all the people and animals that God purposed to save, plus all the supplies they would need for the year they would spend aboard.

Our Lord Jesus is a sufficient redeemer for all who believe. There is nothing lacking in his obedience nor in his atonement.

> The cross on which Jesus died
> Is a shelter in which we can hide;
> And its grace so free is sufficient for me,
> And deep is its fountain, as wide as the sea.

He is able to do all that he promised (Rom. 4:21).
He is able to save to the uttermost all who come (Heb. 7:25).
He is able to keep that which we commit to him (2 Tim. 1:12).
He is able to keep us from falling (Jude 24-25).
He is able to raise us from the dead (Phil. 3:20-21).

3. The ark was a safe refuge able to survive the flood

It was pitched within and without (Gen. 6:14), which made it safe from wind, water and rain. None aboard would perish. The ark was designed by God and provided by God. How could it fail?

In just the same way, our Lord Jesus Christ is a sure foundation, a safe refuge and a secure hiding-place. He cannot fail, nor can those perish for whom he died and for whom he intercedes (John 10:27-30; Rom. 8:38-39). Noah's safety and security did not depend on his seamanship, but on the strength and durability of the ark. In the same way, Christ himself is our hope.

4. The ark had only one door and one window

There was only one door for the tall giraffe and the lowly snail. Even so, Christ is *the door*. He said, 'By me if any man enter in, he shall be saved' (John 10:9). There is only one door for the rich and the poor, for the old and the young, for the Greek and the Jew.

The ark had only one window, and it was not provided for them to see out, but for light to shine in. There is only one light — Christ. He is the light of the world. The glory of God is seen in the face of Christ. He is our light and the revelation of the Father.

5. The ark brought them all safely through the flood

So Christ brings to safety all whom he died to save (John 6:37-45).

> Firm as his throne his gospel stands,
> My Lord, my hope, my trust;
> If I am found in Jesus' hands,
> My soul can never be lost.
> His honour is engaged to keep
> The weakest of his sheep;
> All that his heavenly Father gave,
> His hands securely keep.
> Nor death nor hell shall ever remove
> His people from his breast;
> In the dear bosom of his love,
> They shall for ever rest.

Questions
1. How might we describe Noah's trust in God during the time in the ark?
2. Does this compare with our trust in Christ?
3. What does Noah's safe-keeping in the ark speak of for believers in Christ?

4. Sarah and Hagar — law and grace

Genesis 21:1-14; Galatians 4:21-31

There are no two things in the Bible more different than law and grace, that is, the difference between salvation by our works or salvation by free grace through the obedience and death of our Lord Jesus. The first assignment in learning the gospel is to learn the difference between law and grace. He who learns the lesson well can call himself a theologian.

Paul calls the story of Sarah and Hagar an allegory (Gal. 4:24). All allegory is a story in which the characters are used to picture other real characters and real actions.

God promised Abraham a son by his true wife, Sarah. Time passed and no son was born; so Sarah gave her servant, Hagar, to Abraham to bear him a son. Ishmael was born to Hagar by Abraham. In due time the promised son, Isaac, was born to Sarah. The son of the servant, Hagar, mocked Isaac and proved that the two could not live together; so Hagar and Ishmael had to be put out of the household. Isaac reigned alone as the heir of Abraham.

1. Paul said that these two women represent the two covenants. Hagar, the servant, represents the covenant of law, works and ceremonies from Mt Sinai. In the covenant of law and works God says, 'Do this and live.' Sarah, the true wife of Abraham, represents God's eternal covenant of grace in Christ Jesus. This covenant was first, was from all eternity and was not made between God and men, but between the Father, Son and Holy Spirit (Heb. 7:22; 13:20; John 17:2-3). The covenant of grace says, 'Do this, O Christ, and men shall live.' God gives eternal life without works from men (Rom. 3:19-24).

2. Though Hagar bore the first son, as the covenant of works gave us fallen Adam and a depraved race, yet Sarah was the original and first wife of Abraham, just as the covenant of grace was the first covenant. The covenant of works was revealed first, but before there was ever a sinner, there was a covenant of grace and its surety, Christ Jesus. Jesus Christ was the Lamb slain before the foundation of the world (Rev. 13:8; 17:8; 1 Peter 1:18-21). We were chosen in Christ before the world began (Eph. 1:3-4; 2 Thess. 2:13).

3. Hagar was never intended to be the wife of Abraham, nor was Ishmael that seed which was promised. Hagar was the handmaid of Sarah. So the law was never given nor intended to save anyone. It was only a handmaid to grace to point men to Christ, the seed (Gal. 3:21-29,16). The law properly used is a blessing. It shows our sins, our inability; it shuts men up to Christ. If the law is the servant to grace, that is well and good; but when the law tries to be the master, or on an equal footing with grace, it must go! (Gal. 4:30-31).

4. Hagar was never free and Sarah was never in bondage. The covenant of works and her children are not free. All who live by the law are under the curse (Gal. 3:10-13). But the seed of Abraham by faith are free, for 'If the Son ... shall make you free, ye shall be free indeed' (John 8:36).

5. Hagar must be cast out as well as her son (Heb. 10:1-10). The covenant of works has ceased, being fulfilled by Christ. It cannot have a place in the redemption and reign of Christ Jesus. Nor is he a son of Abraham who is one by flesh or natural birth. He is a son of Abraham who is one by faith in Jesus Christ (Rom. 2:28-29; Gal. 3:7-9,16,29).

6. As the two women are types of the two covenants, so the two sons are types of those who live under each covenant.
Ishmael is the man who trusts his works and seeks a righteousness before God by his deeds. Isaac is the man born supernaturally of God (John 1:13), brought to faith in Christ, who walks in the Spirit, not the flesh, and whose wisdom, righteousness, sanctification and redemption are all to be found in Christ alone (1 Cor. 1:30; Col. 2:9-10).

Ishmael is the older, as the old man is older than the new man created in Christ Jesus. We are all born in the flesh first, then born again with that new nature which lives for ever.

Ishmael is the son of the flesh; Isaac is the son by divine power. We are all born sons of men, then later sons of God.

Ishmael's attitude towards Isaac (Gal. 4:29) is the same attitude that the legalist displays towards sons of grace today. You will never find a free-will legalist to be tolerant towards the gospel of grace. The gospel of grace destroys his very foundation, which is merit, not mercy!

Questions
1. Why is it important to distinguish between law and grace?
2. What is 'the gospel'?
3. What is it to believe the gospel?

5. 'The Lord will provide'

Genesis 22:1-14

Genesis 22 records Abraham's greatest trial and Abraham's greatest revelation of the gospel of Christ (John 8:56). Genesis 22 is full of Christ and could rightly be called 'the gospel of Mt Moriah', which mountain many believe to be Mt Calvary, where Christ died.

v. 1.   The chapter begins with **'after these things'**; that is to say, after nine or ten great trials (the Jews say that Abraham had ten great trials), Abraham was called upon to endure the greatest trial of all — the sacrifice of his only son. Our sovereign God does all things he has purposed to do 'in due time' (Rom. 5:6) and 'in the fulness of time' (Gal. 4:4). 'After these things,' after the Fall, the flood, the exodus, the tabernacle, the prophets and kings, it pleased God to fulfil every promise, prophecy and pattern in the sacrifice of his only-begotten Son. All that had gone before pictured and pointed to this hour when Christ would die (Acts 10:43; Luke 24:27,44-46).

v. 2.   The words of this verse, taken one by one, reveal the greatness of the gift, the love behind it and the agony endured through it. Can you imagine the grief of Abraham when he received this command, the sorrow he suffered in considering the death of his son at his own hand, the great love he revealed in his willingness to give Isaac, or the supreme sacrifice involved?

'**Take ... thy son.**' The Lord Jesus is the Son of God.
'**Thine only son.**' Is he not called 'his only begotten Son'?
'**Whom thou lovest.**' God said, 'This is my beloved Son.'

'And offer him ... for a burnt offering.' Christ Jesus became our burnt offering, our sin offering, our sacrifice by the will of the Father, who was pleased to bruise him (Isa. 53:10; Heb. 10:9-10).

vv. 3-4. Abraham had three full days in which to consider the sacrifice of his son Isaac. As they journeyed through the days and slept through the nights, this burden and sacrifice lay upon his heart. But the eternal Father foreordained and purposed the sacrifice of Christ Jesus, not for three days, or even three thousand days, but before the foundation of the world (Rev. 13:8; Eph. 1:3-4). What love, what grace, and what a sure and certain promise we have in our Lord Jesus Christ and in God's eternal purpose, which has never changed! (Mal. 3:6; Rom. 11:29; Num. 23:19).

vv. 5-6. Abraham carefully prepared all that was involved in the sacrifice — the wood, the sharpened knife and the fire. What shall we say of our great God, who carefully prepared, predestinated and foretold all events, all people, all nations and all actions of the greatest event of all time — the death of Christ? (Acts 2:23; 4:27-28). Abraham commanded his servants to remain at the foot of the mountain and the father and the son went to the mountain together. Redemption is the work of the Father and the Son. 'God was in Christ, reconciling the world unto himself' (2 Cor. 5:19); yet Christ was in the hands of and under the wrath of God for our sins (Isa. 53:4-6). Twelve went with him to the Passover, eleven went with him to the garden, three went with him to pray; but when he went to the cross, he went there alone (Heb. 1:3). Upon Isaac, Abraham laid the wood, even as the cruel cross was laid upon the shoulders of our Lord.

vv. 7-8. As Abraham and Isaac walked up the mountain to offer a sacrifice and to worship God, Isaac asked, **'My father ... behold the fire and the wood: but where is the lamb for a burnt offering?'** Isaac knew that (God being holy, righteous and just, and man being guilty, sinful and evil) there can be no acceptance, no forgiveness, no communion between God and men without the blood (Lev. 17:11; Exod. 12:13; Heb. 9:22). He knew about Cain's error and condemnation. Abraham uttered that great prophecy which is the very heart of all God's purpose, the gospel and our hope. **'My son,**

God will provide himself a lamb for a burnt offering.' He later named the place Jehovah-Jireh — the Lord will see to it, or provide! This prophecy says many things:

> 1. The Lord will provide *himself* as the Lamb, for our Lord Jesus, the Lamb of God, is God!
> 2. The Lord will provide *for* himself a Lamb; for the Lord God is the offended majesty to whom, and for whom, the blood was shed, that he might be both just and justifier (Rom. 3:23-26).
> 3. The Lord will *provide,* or see to it, that redemption for all his sheep, the honouring of his law, the satisfaction of his justice, the fulfilment of his covenant and the eternal glory of his Son is accomplished in full. Nothing will be left undone. 'It is finished,' the Saviour cried — and it is!

v. 9. **'Abraham ... bound Isaac his son, and laid him on the altar.'** Isaac did not resist the will of his father, even as Christ Jesus was willing and obedient even to the death of the cross (Phil. 2:6-8). Christ could not have come, could not have been arrested, could not have been bound to the tree and could not have died, except it had pleased the Father.

vv. 10-13.   Here Isaac, the type of Christ, ends; for Isaac was removed from the altar and a ram took his place, which also is a picture of the Lord Jesus dying for us. The ram pictures Christ, our sacrifice, and Isaac pictures the believer, who is spared.

Questions
1. To what extent might Abraham and Isaac have understood the significance of the day's events as they returned down the mountain? (Consider Heb. 11:17-19).
2. Can you see Christ as your substitute, just as surely as Isaac saw the slain ram where he had recently lain?
3. Discuss some of the aspects of Christ's words: 'It is finished.'

6. A bride for the heir

Genesis 24

No picture or type of Christ is perfect. God uses earthly stories and people to illustrate heavenly truth, and the very fact that the characters are flesh and the incidents take place in the world is enough to make them imperfect illustrations. In this story of Abraham's servant seeking a bride for Isaac (Abraham's son), Abraham represents the heavenly Father; Isaac, the Lord Jesus; the servant, ministers of the gospel (instruments of the Holy Spirit); and Rebekah, every true believer.

vv. 1-4. Abraham was very wealthy and his son, Isaac, was the heir of all things that Abraham possessed. He sent his trusted servant to find a bride for Isaac, a bride who would share with him all the riches and glories of his inheritance.

The Lord Jesus, the only begotten Son of God's love, is the heir of all things. The Father has given all things into his hands (John 3:35; 5:23; Col. 1:16-18). He is Lord and King by design, by decree and by his death (Rom. 14:9; John 17:1-3). God has chosen out of every tribe, kindred and nation a people to be the bride of his Son and joint-heirs with him of all that he purchased and owns (Rom. 8:14-17, 29-31; Eph. 1:3-7).

The Father calls and sends his servants (preachers of the gospel) out into the world to find this bride of Christ (Mark 16:15-16; 2 Cor. 5:18-20; 1 Cor. 1:17-18, 26-31).

vv. 5-9. I am sure that the servant was full of questions about his mission, but the one great question was, 'What if the woman is unwilling to leave her home and family to love, marry and give herself to a man she does not know and has never seen?' Abraham assured the servant that he was not going forth alone but that the Lord God, who made Isaac the heir, would go with him and reward his efforts: **'He shall send his angel before thee.'**

God's preachers do not go forth into the world alone to persuade men to love, believe and come to Christ, by their own logic, power of persuasion and rhetoric. The Spirit of God goes before them to quicken, awaken and give sinners ears to hear the gospel, eyes to see the beauties of Christ and a heart to love him (Ps. 110:3; Eph. 2:1-10). The bride has been chosen (2 Thess. 2:13), the servant will journey and endure all things to tell the bride of her beloved (2 Tim. 2:9-10), the bride will hear the voice of her beloved through the message of the servant (John 10:23-30) and the bride will come (John 6:37-40; 2 Cor. 2:14-16).

vv. 10-14. The servant went to the place where the women came to draw water and, knowing the great responsibility upon him and the impossibility of the task, humanly speaking, sought divine help in sincere prayer.

The opening of the heart to Christ, the resurrection of the spiritually dead, conviction of sin, genuine repentance towards God and faith in the Lord Jesus are 'impossible with men' (Matt. 19:24-26; 1 Cor. 2:9-12). We preach, but the Spirit of God reveals the Lord Jesus to the heart (John 16:13-15). We teach the head, but only the living God can teach the heart (John 6:44-45). All who come to Christ and receive him must be born of God (John 1:10-13), for true repentance and saving faith are the gifts of God (Rom. 2:4; 2 Tim. 2:24-25; Eph. 2:8-9; Phil. 1:29).

vv. 32-51. The servant was welcomed into Rebekah's home, but he would not partake of its comforts until he had accomplished his mission and declared his message. In the same way, the servants of Christ are men on a mission, who care not for the world's comforts and honours, but are taken up with what God called them to do — to make Christ known (Acts 20:33). The servant declared to Rebekah and her kindred the glories of Isaac and his master's house. The servants of Christ have one message — Christ and him crucified (1 Cor. 2:1-2). The bride must not be attracted to the servant, nor to anything he has to offer, but to Christ.

vv. 56-58. Finally, after the case had been fully stated, the question was put directly to Rebekah: **'Wilt thou go?'** And she said, **'I will go.'** Faith in Christ, salvation in Christ and a saving interest in the Lord Jesus is an individual, personal and total commitment. Children cannot be sprinkled into the covenant and kingdom, young people are not saved because their parents know God, wives and husbands do not partake of grace because they are married to believers (remember Lot's wife) and salvation is not the result of group therapy. Knowing the true God and Jesus Christ is a personal experience as God is pleased to reveal himself to an individual (Gal. 1:15-16; 2 Tim. 1:12; Ps. 23).

Questions
1. What does the fact that 'All who come to Christ and receive him must be born of God' teach us about our involvement in our conversion to Christ?
2. What does it teach us about God's involvement?
3. Which person of the Godhead effects this work of rebirth?

7. Bethel — the house of God

Genesis 28:10-22

Blessed is the man who can read the Scriptures and find the key of knowledge — Christ Jesus! 'Had ye believed Moses, ye would have believed me: for he wrote of me,' said the Lord Jesus (John 5:46). God spoke to these Old Testament believers by the prophets, by pictures and types and by dreams and visions, to reveal his redemptive purpose and grace through Christ Jesus.

Jacob is a man difficult to understand, but the one thing we know about this man is that he was one of God's elect and 'God loved him' (Gen. 25:21-23; Rom. 9:10-13; Gen. 35:9-13).

1. His name means 'supplanter', which is someone who takes the place of another through force or plotting (Gen. 27:35-36).

2. He tricked his brother, Esau, into selling him the birthright (Gen. 25:29-34).

3. Through his mother's influence and help, he deceived his father, Isaac, into giving him the blessing reserved for the first-born (Gen. 27:19-24).

4. He had to flee from his father's house and from the wrath of his brother (Gen. 27:41-44).

5. God met Jacob on his flight from Esau; and what a night that was, as God spoke to Jacob, promised his presence and mercies and revealed to Jacob the way to God — Christ Jesus!

vv. 10-11. There is one reason why Jacob is out here in the desert alone, away from his home and family, and fleeing for his life — and that is his sin. What we are (proud, covetous, lonely, unhappy, depressed) and where we are (away from God, under the curse of the law, without strength, help, or hope) is because of our sins. 'Your sins have separated you and your God.' How undeserving and unworthy is Jacob— and all of us Jacobs! As David said, God is just in condemning us and clear when he judges us (Ps. 51:3-4). Every man who is an object of God's love and grace judges himself, stops his mouth and justifies God in his righteous judgements against our sins.

vv. 12-14. The Lord revealed his mercies to Jacob in a dream. What a blessed time it is when the Lord is pleased in his grace to speak to us on our road to destruction and reveal his mercies in Christ Jesus to the chief of sinners! (Eph. 2:1-7; Rom. 5:6-8). Jacob, the sinner, was still and quiet, and God spoke, revealing Christ in the dream.

The *ladder* stood upon the earth, but the top reached to heaven. So Christ Jesus, although he stood on the earth in the flesh, yet he is the Most High God, who never left the bosom of the Father (Phil. 2:6-8; John 1:14).

The *angels* went up and down on the ladder, which declares to us that we are able to ascend to God only in and by Christ Jesus (John 14:6); and it is by and through Christ that God comes to us. 'God was in Christ reconciling the world unto himself' (2 Cor. 5:19).

The *Lord God* stood above the ladder and made all of his rich promises to Jacob; so God in Christ, and through Christ, makes all the promises of spiritual blessings, eternal life and glory to us (Eph. 1:3-7).

v. 15. What God spoke to Jacob in this verse is his promise to all believers in Christ Jesus.

> **'I am with thee,'** in covenant mercies, in redemptive grace and in constant indwelling love (Rom. 8:28-39).
> **'I ... will keep thee.'** None whom God has chosen, for whom Christ died and who is brought by the Spirit to believe will ever perish (John 6:37-45; 10:24-30).
> **'I ... will bring thee ... into this land.'** Canaan is but a type of heaven. Christ, our surety, will bring to glory all of his sheep. In heaven there will be plenty of room, but no vacancies. Every place prepared will be occupied by those for whom it is prepared (John 14:1-3).

'**I will not leave thee, until I have done that which I have spoken to thee of.**' Our Lord will not fail. The pleasure of the Lord shall prosper in his hand (Isa. 53:10-11).

vv. 16-19. Jacob called the place 'Bethel', house of God and gate of heaven. This term cannot be applied to a church building, which men call 'the house of God'. This can only be where God actually dwells. The house of God is where God is, where God dwells and where God reveals himself. The gate of heaven is the door, and Christ said, 'I am the door: by me if any man enter in, he shall be saved.'

vv. 20-22. Jacob responded to God's call, to God's revelation, as all of his called ones respond. 'Thy people shall be willing' (Ps. 110:3). Christ said, 'Other sheep I have, ... them also I must bring, and they shall hear my voice; and there shall be one fold, and one shepherd' (John 10:16). The people of God are not saved against their wills but are made willing (2 Thess. 2:13). No man can, is able, or has the desire, to come to Christ unless he is taught of God, called of God and has learned of God, but those who are called, taught and drawn to Christ *shall* come (John 6:44-45).

Questions
1. How have our sins separated us from God?
2. Christ is called our mediator in 1 Timothy 2:5. How does the picture of 'Jacob's ladder' assist us to understand this aspect of Christ's work for us?
3. Consider the promises in v.15. Apply each of them to the believer in Christ. What confidences do such promises inspire?

8. Peniel — the face of God

Genesis 32:24-32

v. 24. **'And Jacob was left alone.'** Was there ever a man more troubled, more frightened and confused, more alone than Jacob at this time? His whole life had been one of trouble and disappointment.

    1. He was born second to Esau. He was inferior to Esau. His father preferred Esau.

    2. Pushed by his mother to deceive his blind father, he had stolen the birthright.

    3. Threatened with death by his brother, he fled from his country.

    4. God met him at Bethel, promised his blessings and confirmed what, I am sure, his mother had told him (Gen. 25:22-23; Rom. 9:10-13).

    5. He had been deceived by Laban, as he had deceived Isaac, and married a woman he did not want (Gen. 29:16-26).

    6. He was told by God to return home (Gen. 31:3).

    7. On his journey home he was told that Esau, his brother, was coming to meet him with 400 men (Gen. 32:6-8).

Now Jacob is alone, afraid and helpless. There is no more time nor room for plotting, scheming and manipulating. He is shut up to the sovereign power and deliverance of God. Like Israel at the sea and Jonah in the whale, his salvation is totally in the hands of God (Jonah 2:9; Exod. 14:13). Those whom the Lord is pleased to save and to whom he will reveal his mercy in Christ Jesus will all be brought to the place of human helplessness and inability. There must be left no room for boasting nor glorying in the flesh (Ps. 107:1-6,11-13; 1 Cor. 1:26-31).

'There wrestled a man with him.' Who was this man? There is no doubt that it was Christ, who frequently appeared in human form to saints of the Old Testament, in token and pledge of his future incarnation (Heb. 7:1-3). Verses 26, 28 and 30 reveal who the man is.

Jacob, being an object of God's love and mercy, was laid hold of by the Lord Jesus in sovereign power and purpose (Rom. 8:29-31); Jacob, in his loneliness, fear and need, laid hold of Christ. This was a physical, mental and spiritual conflict which had to be resolved. God is sovereign and man is responsible; God will have his people and his people will have their God (John 6:37-39). The Lord is King by right, by decree and by his death, but he will be the King in the hearts of his people by true submission and surrender (Ps. 110:3; Rom. 10:9-10). They wrestled 'until the breaking of the day'. This was no brief and passing encounter, not an indifferent decision at the front of a church. Great issues are at stake; eternal matters will be resolved right here as Christ personally meets Jacob. God will bless and use Jacob, but it will be a conquered, subdued and surrendered Jacob.

v. 25. 'When he saw that he prevailed not against [Jacob], he touched the hollow of his thigh' and crippled him. There is no question but that the Lord could easily have subdued Jacob. The conflict was ordered by God and the outcome was not in doubt. But God's people are not puppets nor robots, and through his revelation, trials and dealings with them, they must see, feel and experience the frailty of flesh, the emptiness of this world and the glory of God in Christ, and must desire *above all things* his salvation and his presence. Finally, the Lord struck a crippling blow and Jacob went down.

v. 26. He had touched Jacob and would leave, but Jacob held on, crying for the Lord's blessing and power. 'I will not let thee go, except thou bless me.' He had had an unusual revelation, he had wrestled with God, he had been wounded; but the battle was not over for Jacob until he was assured of the Lord's permanent blessing upon him and his peace within him. This was life or death for Jacob — a battle that would not be fought again. He had heard promises of God's blessings; now he wanted them in truth. He was still Jacob, his past clouded with sin. He was a wanderer in a strange country and must still face Esau, his angry brother. He knew he was no better off for this experience unless the Lord gave him his approval, acceptance and presence.

vv. 27-28. Our Lord asked, **'What is thy name?'** He said, **'Jacob'** — cheat, supplanter, deceiver, holder of the birthright by human effort. He had laid claim to the blessing by his mother's and his own decision and deception; now he wanted the blessing from God by God's will and purpose! The Lord changed his name to Israel, a prince who has power (acceptance, union and sonship) with God. This position is not one achieved by merit, works, nor human will, but by his grace (John 1:11-13; Rom. 9:15-16; Eph. 1:3-7).

v. 29. Jacob asked, 'What is your name?' The Lord replied, 'Why do you ask my name?' We can only speculate, but ...

1. Human curiosity has a way of prying into things God has not volunteered.
2. Perhaps Jacob looked for proof and signs. Is not God's word enough?
3. Maybe there was a little pride and ambition to be on a first-name basis with God.
4. One thing is certain — Jacob would not be carried beyond the bounds of faith prescribed for the age in which he lived. We believe God as he has been pleased to reveal himself to us, and true faith demands nothing more.

v. 30. Jacob called the place 'Peniel' — the face of God; for he said, **'I have seen God face to face.'**

1. This was no mere emotional experience; he had met Christ.
2. No soul-winner nor preacher told him that he was saved; he had personally encountered the Redeemer himself.
3. He knew that his life was preserved by the will and act of God, who could justly have destroyed him (Rom. 8:33-34). He had met God and came away preserved — what a small matter it was now to meet Esau!

Questions

1. Human helplessness and inability afflict every sinner. What does this mean?

2. Crippled and helpless by the hand of God, Jacob pleaded for blessing. How might we apply this to a Christian's conversion experience?

3. Jacob's walk was changed for ever following his encounter with Christ. Was it obedience to a set of rules, or a personal contact with Christ which made the difference? Explain this.

9. Joseph opens the storehouses

Genesis 41

Joseph had been sold into slavery by his jealous brothers, who resented Jacob's great love for him (Gen. 37:3-4) and the dreams Joseph had in which God revealed that his brethren would one day bow to and serve him (Gen. 37:5-8). As a result of several acts of God's providence, Joseph wound up in prison in Egypt, where he met the chief butler of Pharaoh's court and interpreted his dream. Later, when Pharaoh had a dream which no one could interpret, the chief butler remembered the young Hebrew, Joseph (Gen. 41:9-14), and he was called before Pharaoh to interpret his dream. God revealed to Joseph that there would be seven years of plenty in the land, followed by seven years of great famine (Gen. 41:28-32). Pharaoh appointed Joseph to be the ruler over all Egypt, second only to himself (Gen. 41:39-44).

There are so many lessons to be learned from this story:

    1. The sovereign providence and divine purpose of God in the life of Joseph, bringing him from a Hebrew shepherd boy to the throne of Egypt. God ruled and overruled all events, all creatures and all their actions to accomplish his will and purpose towards Joseph (Gen. 45:5; 50:20; Isa. 46:9-11; Acts 4:26-28; John 6:37-39).

    2. The sovereignty of God, not only over men, but over the weather, crops, heathen nations and even over men's dreams.

3. The faithfulness of God's servant, Joseph. In the greatest trials, adversity and surroundings, Joseph walked with God and maintained a strong testimony to truth and grace. Even in a heathen nation, Joseph glorified God and God blessed him.

But this entire story, as all Scripture, is given to praise, exalt and reveal our Lord Jesus Christ in his redemptive work (Luke 24:27,44-45).

During the seven years before the famine, Joseph supervised the crops and filled the storehouses, and when there was famine over all the land, Joseph opened the storehouses and sold unto all who had need (v. 56).

1. Joseph opened the storehouses by royal authority

Pharaoh gave all things (all authority and all the food) into the hands of Joseph (vv. 41, 44-45). When people came to Pharaoh, he sent them to Joseph. By God's royal decree and design, all things pertaining to life, salvation, mercy and heaven have been given into the hands of the Lord Jesus Christ (John 3:35-36; 17:2-3; Col. 1:14-19; 2:9-10).

What? All spiritual blessings, all fulness.
Where? In Christ Jesus (Eph. 1:3-4).
Why? Because it pleased God (Col. 1:19).

2. Joseph was the only fit person to open the storehouses

Joseph prophesied the famine; no one else knew about it. Joseph planned the crops and the storehouses (v. 35). Joseph gathered the corn and stored it up (v. 49).

Our Lord Jesus is the only fit and qualified one to open the storehouse of mercy to sinners.

He foreknew the Fall and famine of human nature (Rom. 5:12,19).

He purposed and planned the everlasting covenant of mercy whereby a people would be saved from Adam's race (Heb. 13:20-21).

He came to earth in the likeness of human flesh and obeyed the law in order that his people might have a perfect righteousness before God's law, and he died on the cross that they might all be justified in God's sight. He filled the storehouse with grace and mercy for all who would come to eat; as the disciples replied, 'Lord, to whom shall we go? Thou hast the words of eternal life.'

He is the only one who has the capacity to contain all the fulness of God, the only one who has the wisdom to distribute the fulness of God and the only one who can continue eternally to be our fulness (2 Tim. 1:12; Phil. 3:20-21).

3. *Joseph opened the storehouses*

That is why Joseph filled the storehouses — in order that the people might eat. That is why Christ became our surety and our sin-offering — in order that sinners might be saved (Matt. 1:21; 1 Tim. 1:15; Luke 19:10).

To have kept the storehouses closed would have brought no glory to Joseph nor good to the people. He had plenty and was delighted to distribute it. Our Lord is plenteous in mercy, and he delights to show mercy. His chief glory is his goodness (Exod. 33:18-19). He says, 'Ho, every one that thirsteth, come ... to the waters' (Isa. 55:1; John 7:37-38).

Joseph opened the storehouses at a fit time. When the people cried for bread, Joseph opened the storehouses. All who are hungry will be fed (Rom. 10:13; Gal. 1:15).

Joseph opened the storehouses to all who came (v. 57). Not the Egyptians only, but all nations came to Joseph. Our Lord Jesus opens the storehouses of grace to Jew and Gentile, male and female, bond and free. 'Whosoever will, let him take the water of life' (Rev. 22:17; Matt. 11:28). As the famine is universal, the command to repent and come to Christ is universal. He is able to save to the uttermost *all* who come to God by him (Heb. 7:25).

Questions
1. What does John 14:6 reveal about Christ, the only fit person to be our Saviour?

2.   God has a purpose, a plan and a people. How has Christ achieved all of these?

3.   Consider Hebrews 7:25. What does it reveal of the breadth and narrowness of salvation?

10. Joseph and his brothers

Genesis 42-45

God, in his wisdom, uses the natural world, creatures and events to illustrate the spiritual world, his saving grace and his redemptive work in Christ Jesus. The wonders which God performs in the heart can be seen in the wonders he performs upon earth and records in his Word (1 Cor. 10:4; John 3:14; Matt. 12:40). It is the duty of the preacher and the teacher to look for these parables and pictures and preach Christ from them. Joseph's dealings with his brothers are a picture of our Lord's dealings with his erring brethren, given him by the Father and purchased with his blood.

41:57. **'The famine was ... in all lands.'** The terrible famine was not only over the land of Egypt, but over all lands and reached to all people. There was no food even in Israel, the chosen people.

This is what the Word of God declares concerning sin and spiritual death. It is a famine of sin and spiritual death which is over all of Adam's race, even the elect of God.

'Death passed upon all men, for that all have sinned' (Rom. 5:12).

'For all have sinned, and come short of the glory of God' (Rom. 3:23).

'We ... were by nature the children of wrath, even as others' (Eph. 2:3).

'Ye were without Christ ... having no hope, and without God' (Eph. 2:12).

42:1. Jacob heard some good news: 'There is corn in Egypt.' Jacob called his sons together to tell them the good news: 'We do not have to die, for I have heard that there is plenty of corn in Egypt.'

This is the good news of the gospel preached to hungry, weary and dying sinners — we do not have to continue in spiritual poverty, hunger and death; for there is life, mercy and grace in Christ Jesus.

> 'If any man thirst, let him come unto me and drink' (John 7:37).
> 'He hath filled the hungry with good things' (Luke 1:53).
> 'I am that bread of life ... which cometh down from heaven, that a man may eat thereof, and not die' (John 6:48-40).

Jacob could not be sure that the rumour he had heard about corn in Egypt was true, but we can be sure the bread of life and the water of life in Christ is true because we have the sure Word of God (1 John 5:9-11).

Jacob did not know that his own son was in charge of the corn in Egypt; therefore, he might have entertained doubts that he could buy food there. But we can be sure that all who come for mercy and grace will be received and blessed, for our heavenly Father has given all things to Christ, our Saviour, brother and friend, who loves us and gave himself for us!

Jacob was not sure that he could get enough food for such a large family. There were seventy of them. But we know that our Lord's grace is sufficient to save to the uttermost all who come to God by him (Isa. 1:18; 1 John 1:7-9; Matt. 11:28).

Jacob sent money to Egypt to buy corn. God's grace is free. 'All the fitness [Christ] requireth is to feel your need of him' (see Isa. 55:1-3).

42:1-2. 'Why do you hesitate? Why do you stand looking at one another? Get down to Egypt and buy food that we may live and not die!'

This is the urgent, immediate command of the gospel. You are a sinner, you have no life nor hope in yourself nor in another; if you remain where you are, you will perish for ever. There is life in Christ Jesus, who, of God, is made unto us all we need (1 Cor. 1:30; Col. 2:9-10). Come to Christ, flee to Christ, believe on Christ (Isa. 45:20-25; John 5:39-40).

Read Genesis 42-44 and study the dealings Joseph had with his brothers, who had hated him without a cause, who had sold him into slavery, who had dealt so harshly and cruelly with him. Their sin must be revealed to them, and they must own their guilt (42:21-23). These proud brothers must be humbled before him, bow down and plead for mercy (44:14). There must be evidence of genuine repentance (44:33-34).

Is this not a picture of God's dealing with all whom he saves?

1. Our sinful nature, and even the corruption of our best deeds are brought before us (1 John 1:8-10; Isa. 64:6). We own our guilt of unbelief and our part in Adam's fall and the crucifixion of God's dear Son (Isa. 53:1-3).

2. We come hungry, empty and needy before God's throne of grace, confessing our sins and owning God's justice in condemning us (Ps. 51:3-4). We fall at the feet of Christ Jesus, whom we denied, rejected and crucified, and own that he is Lord and can do with us what he will (Matt. 8:1-2; Rom. 10:9-10; Phil. 2:9-11).

3. This is not outward form, nor ritual, nor feigned repentance. Like Judah of old, we are genuinely pleading for his mercy to the undeserving and waiting upon the Lord. Salvation is in him, of him, and his to give. He can justly condemn us or mercifully save us. We have no claim on him; nor is he obligated to help us, only as he is faithful to his covenant in Christ.

45:1-5. In due time Joseph revealed himself to his brothers and spoke peace to them. Christ will in due time reveal himself to sincere seekers and speak peace to their hearts (John 6:37-45).

Questions
1. Why is physical famine a good analogy for spiritual famine?
2. The gospel points to Christ, 'the bread of life'. How is this picture continued when believers gather to break bread at the Lord's Supper?
3. Why is breaking bread, a family meal, only for believers?

11. Shiloh

Genesis 49:8-10

Before the written Word was given, God spoke to the fathers in various ways about the coming Messiah. Who can say what Abel understood as he, by faith, brought the blood sacrifice? Who knows what Enoch understood (Jude 14), or Abraham, of whom Christ said, 'He rejoiced to see my day'?

In this chapter the dying Jacob (Israel) called his twelve sons together for the purpose of prophesying future things relating to the twelve tribes which descended from them. He had a word for all of them, but Judah is praised and good things are prophesied of him, particularly that 'Shiloh', or the Messiah, should spring from him. From the tribe of Judah came David, Solomon and the Lord Jesus. The Israelites are called Jews. Over Christ's cross was written, 'Jesus of Nazareth, King of the Jews', and Paul wrote, 'He is a Jew, which is one inwardly' (Rom. 2:28-29). What Jacob said of Judah, he spoke with regard to the Lord Jesus.

v. 8. **'Thou art he whom thy brethren shall praise.'** The name Judah means 'praise'. His mother gave him that name when he was born and said, 'Now will I praise the Lord' (Gen. 29:35). Christ Jesus, our Messiah and King, is worthy of, deserves and shall have the sincere praise of his people.

> Now to the Lord, that makes us know
> The wonders of his eternal love,
> Be humble honours paid below
> And strains of nobler praise above.

To Jesus our atoning priest,
To Jesus our superior King,
Be everlasting praise confessed,
And every tongue his glories sing.

Nothing is more inconsistent with faith than murmuring and unhappiness.

'**Thy hand shall be in the neck of thine enemies.**' When someone has his hands securely on the neck of his enemies, he can stop their breath and destroy them. Christ will be victorious over his enemies (Heb. 1:13).

1. Our Lord met Satan and defeated him.
2. Our Lord took our sins to the cross and conquered.
3. Our Lord met death, lay in a tomb and arose triumphantly.
4. There is no enemy of his, his people, nor his kingdom that shall not finally be destroyed.

'**Thy Father's children shall bow down before thee.**' It is true that the nation of Israel bowed down before David and Solomon and the Kings of Judah, and this prophecy refers immediately to that; but the greater honour and glory is reserved for David's son, before whom not only believers shall bow, but the entire universe (Phil. 2:9-11). He is Lord by his deity, by the Father's design and decree, and he is Lord by death (Rom. 14:9; 10:9-10).

v. 9. '**Judah is a lion's whelp.**' The Lord Jesus is compared to a young lion because of his strength, power and courage. The lion is called the king of the jungle; our Lord is called 'the Lion of the tribe of Judah' (Rev. 5:5).

'**From the prey, my son, thou art gone up.**' He left heaven and came to this earth to engage the enemy and redeem a people by his mighty arm. He has accomplished that work ('It is finished') and ascended to the right hand of majesty.

'**He stooped down.**' Was there ever such a stoop as this? He made himself of no reputation, took on himself the form of a servant. He became obedient unto death, even the death of the cross (Phil. 2:7-8).

'**As an old lion, who shall rouse him up?**' He stooped, he conquered, he arose, he ascended, he sat down, having accomplished his pleasure. Who shall disturb him? Who shall question him? Who shall interfere or stand against him? Like an old lion who has killed and devoured his prey, who shall rouse him?

v. 10. **'The sceptre shall not depart from Judah ... until Shiloh come.'** Here is the great and glad word! Here is the great prophecy: the Messiah will come through the tribe of Judah, the family of Jesse and the house of David. Where did Jacob get the name Shiloh? God gave him a special name for a special person and a special time. Here are some of the meanings given to the word by various writers:

1. Shiloh means *'sent'* (John 9:7). Some point out the likeness between Siloam and Shiloh. Christ is truly the sent one: 'As my Father sent me ...'
2. Shiloh means the *'son'*, others say (Isa. 9:6-7). He is the true Son of God, the Son of David and the Son of Man.
3. Shiloh means *'the one to whom it belongs'* (Ezek. 21:25-27). The sceptre, the crown, the throne and the worship belong to him. All others are impostors (Col. 1:14-18).
4. Shiloh means *peace*. It is said that the word comes from the same word as 'Salem', or 'peace' (Heb. 7:2). The Lord Jesus is our peace (Rom. 5:1). He made peace through the blood of his cross.

'Unto him shall the gathering of the people be.' The object of his covenant, his cross and his coming to earth was to redeem a people and gather them to himself for ever. They shall come! In repentance, faith and love, they shall come! (John 6:37-39; 10:14-16; 17:1-10).

Questions
1. Christ alone is the focus of our worship. Why?
2. How does a true understanding of the glory of Christ equip a believer for daily living?
3. Reflect on how Genesis 49:10 is at one time a prophecy and a promise.

12. The Passover

Exodus 12:1-13

The Lord had sent plague after plague upon the Egyptians, but each time Pharaoh's heart was hardened, and he would not allow the Israelites to leave Egypt. The Lord spoke to Moses (Exod. 11:1) and declared that he would bring one more plague upon Egypt; after that plague, Pharaoh would send them forth out of the land.

The Passover lamb is a special type of Christ, perhaps the clearest and most complete of all the types and pictures, for in it the Lord God preached to the Jews the whole doctrine of the gospel: in the choice of the sacrifice (John 1:29); in the characteristics of the lamb (1 Peter 2:22); in the death of the lamb and the sprinkling of the blood (Heb. 9:11-14); in the eating of the lamb and the faith that rested (John 6:53-54); in the grand results of it all — the people were delivered and God was glorified (Exod. 12:26-27; Eph. 3:21).

One of the best ways to study the Passover as a picture and type of Christ is to look at the parallels between this Passover and 'Christ, our Passover, [who] is sacrificed for us' (1 Cor. 5:7).

1. *The lamb was to be without blemish.* This signifies the absolute perfection and sinlessness of our Lord Jesus (Heb. 4:15; 2 Cor. 5:21). The Lord Jesus, in order to be our righteousness, must live a perfect life; and in order to atone for our sin, he must have no sin of his own. The sacrifice 'shall be perfect to be accepted' (Lev. 22:21).

2. *The lamb was to be taken out of the fold.* Jesus Christ, our Lamb, was taken from among men (Deut. 18:15-19). He was the seed of

woman, the seed of Abraham (Gal. 3:16), and made of the seed of David according to the flesh (Rom. 1:3).

3. *The lamb was to be a year old and was to be killed,* showing that our Lord in his full strength of life should be put to death.

4. *The lamb was to be roasted with fire,* which probably signifies the manner of Christ's death. He was crucified, enduring the fire of God's wrath for our sins and the burning fever of his wounds.

5. *The lamb was to be roasted whole,* not a bone broken, as the Scriptures declare of Christ (John 19:36).

6. *The blood of the lamb must be sprinkled* upon the lintel and the sides of the door of the Israelites, as the blood of Christ is applied by faith. There is no salvation nor deliverance apart from faith (John 3:36). God did not put the blood on the door; the people put it there, believing God (Heb. 11:6). The blood on the door denotes an outward confession and evidence of heart faith. In all our going out and going in, the blood of the Lamb is before us.

7. *The Israelites were to eat the flesh of the lamb,* which signifies that we must by faith feed upon Christ. Truly believing on Christ and receiving Christ within us is called eating his flesh and drinking his blood (John 6:55-58).

8. *They were to eat the lamb with unleavened bread.* Leaven is a type of evil. This is to signify that those who come to Christ, the true Passover, are to come in sincerity and truth, hating evil and hypocrisy. They were also to eat the lamb with bitter herbs, which probably shows the sorrow for sin and repentance in the hearts of those who come to Christ. The lamb was not to be eaten raw nor sodden with water; that is, not boiled in wine, oil, or water. Christ endured the full wrath and judgement for our full justification; and nothing is to be mixed, added, nor joined to him.

9. *Nothing of the lamb was to remain.* This says that the whole Christ is to be received and fed upon by faith — Christ in both natures, divine and human; Christ in all his offices, Prophet, Priest and King; Christ in all his person and work.

10. *They were to eat the Passover dressed and ready to move out of Egypt.* This is the Lord's Passover and effectually saves. The world, as Egypt to Israel, is no longer our home. We are pilgrims, temporarily here but awaiting his call to move out and go home to Canaan.

11. **'When I see the blood I will pass over you'** (v. 13). This is why the ordinance was called the Passover, because the Lord, at the sight of the blood of the lamb, passed over the Israelites and delivered them. His judgement and wrath pass over us because of the blood of Christ (Rom. 8:1; Eph. 1:7).

Questions
1. In what ways can the sacrificed lamb be considered as a substitute for the first-born sons in the families of Israel?
2. How has Christ become a substitute for his people before God?
3. As a believer's substitute, Christ took our sins and became our righteousness. In the light of this, what is a believer's standing before God?

13. The manna

Exodus 16:11-18,31; John 6:28-35,48-51

Would we be faithful ministers of the gospel of Christ? Would we be faithful teachers and preachers in our generation? Would we be faithful students and rightly divide the Word of truth? Then we shall search the Old Testament Scriptures and preach Christ from the types, patterns and prophecies, as did our Lord and the disciples (Luke 24:26-27,44-47; 1 Cor. 10:4; 5:7).

In John 6 our Lord refers to the manna which fell in the wilderness and calls himself **'the true bread from heaven'**. In Revelation 2:17 John writes, 'To him that overcometh will I give to eat of the hidden manna.' How is the manna which God gave to Israel a picture of our Lord Jesus Christ, 'the true bread'?

1. Manna was a strange and mysterious thing to the Israelites. They had never seen anything like it before and said to one another, 'What is this?' (Exod. 16:15).

Nothing is more mysterious and wonderful than the incarnation of God in human flesh (1 Tim. 3:16). He who made the world was in the world (John 1:10). He who made woman was made of a woman (Gal. 4:4-5). The living God became a man and dwelt among us, numbered with transgressors, subject to every trial and temptation of the flesh, yet without sin (John 1:14; Heb. 4:14-16). Without the aid of men (no ploughing, no planting, no reaping) the bread lay upon the ground. Even so, without the aid of men the Son of God was conceived and born into the world (Isa. 7:14; Luke 1:30-35).

2. *Manna was prepared in heaven and came down to earth* (Num. 11:9). The people of Israel must have food. It was impossible for them to provide for themselves in the wilderness, so their bread was prepared in heaven and sent down to earth.

Christ Jesus had a body prepared by the Father that he might be food for believers (Heb. 10:5). In the wilderness of flesh and sin there is no food. 'In the flesh dwelleth no good thing.' That which is impossible with men is possible with God.' All the nourishment Israel needed was found in the manna from heaven, and all that a believer needs is in Christ (1 Cor. 1:30; Col. 2:9-10).

3. *Manna was a gift;* it cost them nothing. All they needed to do was to gather it and eat it. Christ Jesus is the unspeakable gift of God's love (2 Cor. 9:15; Rom. 6:23). Our Lord said to the Samaritan woman, 'If you knew the gift of God, you would ask and I would give.' The bread of life, Christ Jesus, is free. That for which men labour never satisfies and in the end will cost them dearly (Isa. 55:1-3).

4. *Manna was provided for all who were hungry* (Exod. 16:16-18). The poor and the rich, the young and the old, male and female, leaders and followers — all had one thing in common. They were hungry, and the manna met everyone's need. All men, of whatever distinction, have one thing in common — all have sinned and all need the Saviour. He is the only Saviour and the only bread (Matt. 11:28; John 6:53-54).

The Israelites gathered the manna daily, and the man who gathered much had nothing over, while he who gathered little had no lack. We feed on Christ daily, coming to him continually for nourishment (1 Peter 2:2-5). There is not a day without a fresh feeding upon him; and whether we have strong faith (the one who gathered much), we have none over, or weak faith (the one who gathered less), we have no lack of nourishment and life. He is sufficient!

5. *Manna was pleasant to the taste* (Exod. 16:31). How sweet and satisfying is the Lord Jesus to those who taste him! His word is sweeter than the honeycomb (Ps. 34:8). He becomes all things to those who believe, meeting their every need.

6. In many ways the manna in the wilderness does *not* picture Christ:

> Manna was food for the outward man only. Christ is the bread of life for the inward man.
> The manna was eaten by those who later died. We eat of Christ and never die.
> The manna rotted and decayed when kept. Christ ever lives! He abides the same yesterday, today and for ever.
> The manna was only found in the morning. Christ is our food morning, noon and night.
> The manna ceased when they entered Canaan. Christ, our bread, is our bread for ever. In glory he will be the subject of our song, the joy of our heart and the object of our worship.

Go worship at Emmanuel's feet
See in his face all wonders meet!
The whole creation can afford
But some faint shadow of my Lord.
Is he compared to wine and bread?
Dear Lord, our souls would thus be fed!
Is he a tree? Then we receive
Salvation from his healing leaves!
Is he a rose? Not Sharon yields
Such fragrancy in all her fields!
Is he the vine? His heavenly root
Supplies the branch with life and fruit!
Is he the fountain? There I bathe
And heal the plague of sin and death.
Is he a fire? He will purge my dross
So the true gold sustains no loss!
Is he the rock? How firm he proves!
The Rock of Ages never moves.
Is he the way that leads to God?
There would I walk in lines of blood!
Is he the door? I'll enter in
To feed on pastures large and green!
Is he the temple? I'll adore
The indwelling majesty and power!

Is he the sun? His beams are grace,
His course is joy and righteousness!
His beauties we can never trace
Till we behold him face to face!

Questions

1. The barren wilderness brought the bitterness of empty stomachs. Manna was sweet and gave hope. How does Christ sweeten and lighten the troubles of our daily life?
2. Without manna the people would die. How does this compare with a sinner's condition without Christ?
3. Strong faith or weak, Christ is sufficient! How does this emphasize God's grace?

14. Water from the rock

Exodus 17:1-7; Matthew 16:18; 1 Corinthians 10:4

The people of Israel journeyed from the wilderness of Sin and pitched in Rephidim. There was no water to drink. The people murmured against Moses because there was no water.

If we did not know something of the evil of the human heart from Scripture (Jer. 17:9) and from our own experience (Rom. 7:24), we should be at a loss to account for the unbelief, ingratitude and insensibility of these people to God's goodness and faithfulness. They had been delivered from Egypt. They had seen the hand of God at the Red Sea. They had been fed with quail and manna. Now they were ready to stone Moses because they had no water.

We learn from Israel in the wilderness a needed lesson, and that is the unvarying tendency of the human heart to doubt God! The smallest cloud of trouble is sufficient to hide the face of God. We had rather lean on a cobweb of human resources and wisdom than on the everlasting, omnipotent arm of God. It is well called 'an evil heart, always ready to depart from the living God'.

Note, if you will, the age-old questions in Exodus 16 and 17: 'What shall we eat? What shall we drink?' The only question missing is, 'What shall we wear?' After these things do the heathen seek.

Faith has a brief but comprehensive answer to all these questions — God! There is nothing that exceeds the wickedness of the human heart except the abounding grace of God! The only thing greater than our sin is his grace! Someone once said, 'Two things man has never fathomed — the depth of sin and the grace of God.'

vv. 4-6. God told Moses, 'Go out, take the elders and your rod. I will stand upon the rock in Horeb. You are to smite the rock. There shall come water out of the rock. The people will drink.'

What makes this event so special? What is there about the smitten rock that is so special? Paul answers in four words: 'That rock was Christ' (1 Cor. 10:4).

1. The people thought that they would perish

All hope was gone, the simple fact being that there was no water. No water means no life. Is this not our state and condition by birth, nature and practice? No spiritual water, no life — only death in a dry, thirsty and barren land (Ps. 63:1-2). The human well is dry, the religious well is dry, the philosopher's well is dry. There is nothing that we can do, nor the world of flesh can do, to save our souls.

2. There is a rock

There is a rock in a weary land;
Its shadows fall on the burning sand.

In appearance it is only a rock like so many other rocks. Without anointed eyes one would never see it, or know the power, beauty and life-giving water therein. Christ said to the woman, 'If you knew, you would ask and I would give you living water.'

Look at the rock! A rock is an unlikely thing to afford water. It was only a rock, yet God stood on that rock. Christ was called 'only a carpenter'; there was no beauty that we should desire him: 'You are only a man; how can you be God?' Oh, for anointed eyes to see that 'God was in Christ'! (2 Cor. 5:19). 'He that hath seen me hath seen the Father' (John 14:9).

3. The rock was smitten

There was no water coming forth from the rock until Moses smote it with his rod. So our Lord Jesus Christ was smitten, scourged and crucified that his precious blood might flow forth for the redemption of our souls. He was 'smitten of God, and afflicted' (Isa. 53:4,10-12). You may get as technical as you wish, but the message of the

Word is clear: 'He was smitten and afflicted' by the wrath, judgement and justice of God for us and '[By] his stripes we are healed' (Isa. 53:4-5).

4. The rock was smitten for a rebellious people

There is no need to dress up Israel. They were a sinful, undeserving people, as we are; they were thirsty, as we are; they could do nothing about it, as we cannot. God had mercy upon them, as he did upon us, and gave them water and life from the rock, as he has given us life in Christ. The rock yielded water abundantly. It required no purification by men, no effort to pipe it, only to drink of it freely. 'All the fitness he requireth is to feel your need of him.'

5. The rock followed them

It followed them through the wilderness, over the hills and valleys to Canaan (1 Cor. 10:4). All the desert could not dry up that rock. So Christ is our fountain of life and the source of all grace through the wilderness of this world until we come to the heavenly Canaan. Also read Numbers 20:1-12.

Questions

1. List some practical ways to deal with our natural tendency to doubt and murmur against God.
2. As the life-giving water from the rock was hidden from the people until it was revealed by God, so we require spiritual eyes to see and spiritual ears to hear Christ. Think about this and read 1 Corinthians 2:14.
3. The rock must be smitten for life to flow out. Christ was smitten by God. Why was this essential for the salvation of sinners?

15. The blood before the Lord

Leviticus 4:1-7

All through the Scriptures we meet with the blood (Exod. 12:13; Lev. 17:11; Heb. 9:22; 1 Peter 1:18-19). If we have any apologies to make in reference to sermons on the blood of Christ, it is that we do not preach on it as often as we should.

What does the shedding of blood mean in reference to sin-offerings and sacrifices in the Scriptures? It means not merely suffering, which could be typified by blood, but it means 'suffering unto death'.

Sin deserves death! The punishment for sin is not discomfort but death. 'In the day that thou eatest thereof thou shalt surely die' (Gen. 2:17). 'The soul that sinneth, it shall die' (Ezek. 18:4,20). 'The wages of sin is death' (Rom. 6:23).

Christ, our Redeemer and substitute, must suffer unto death! The only way that God can honour his holy law, satisfy his perfect justice, fulfil his righteous sentence and yet forgive and justify guilty sinners was for Christ Jesus, the God-man, to come into this world and suffer unto death for us (Rom. 3:25-26; Gal. 3:13; 2 Cor. 5:21; 1 Peter 2:24; 3:18).

All of these blood sacrifices under the law of Moses were typical of the sacrifice of our Lord Jesus in the place and stead of sinners (Luke 24:45-47; Isa. 53:4-6).

The animals sacrificed were always of a tame sort, not wild beasts which by force are brought to the slaughter; for Christ shed his blood and laid down his life willingly (Isa. 53:7).

The animals must be young males, signifying the strength and excellence of Christ; and they must be without spot or blemish, which shows the holiness of Christ (1 Peter 1:18-19; Heb. 9:14).

The blood of the sin-offering was to be poured out, showing how the blood of Christ, our true sin-offering, should be poured forth (John 19:34).

1. *The blood was shed before the Lord*

Note in these brief verses how many times the blood is said to be 'before the Lord'. Whether any man saw it or not was of small account, for it was before the Lord. When the Passover lamb was slain in Egypt, where was the blood placed? It was on the outside of the door, before the Lord. He said, 'When I see the blood, I will pass over you.'

The suffering and death of Christ on behalf of his people was before the Lord, unto the Lord, to declare his righteousness, to honour his holiness, to satisfy his justice, to fulfil his purpose, to glorify his divine character, to enable God to be both just and justifier (Isa. 45:21; Rom. 3:26).

The atonement does not change the nature and character of God, for God is unchangeable; but rather it honours and magnifies the character of God. The death of Christ is not the *cause* of God's love but the *result* of it (John 3:16). God is not merciful to sinners because Christ died; Christ died because God is merciful (Exod. 33:18-19). God is love, God is merciful and gracious; but God is holy, just and righteous. In order that every attribute might be expressed, glorified and honoured, God gave his Son, Jesus Christ, to be the sacrifice and sin-offering of a chosen people.

2. *The blood was brought into the tabernacle and placed on the altar, giving power to the intercession of the priest*

The priest laid his hands on the head of the bullock (v. 4), signifying that our sins are laid on Christ and that we lay the hand of faith upon him.

The shedding of actual blood shows Christ's oneness with us. Has Jesus Christ human blood? Yes, he is truly man, and as a man, he died.

The shedding of his blood shows the full payment of the debt. His blood is no longer in his veins; it is on the altar.

The blood of the bullock was brought into the tabernacle,

showing that our Lord Jesus entered into heaven by his own blood, having obtained eternal redemption for us (Heb. 9:12).

The priest sprinkled the blood seven times before the Lord, showing the perfection of Christ's sacrifice, the number seven being the number of perfection. Christ's death is effectual and sufficient (Eph. 1:7).

The altar of sweet incense (v. 7) is a type of the intercession of Christ on behalf of his people. The sweet incense represents the prayers and intercession of Christ, and the blood on that altar signifies the power of that intercession! He pleads his blood and sacrifice (Rom. 8:34). The cancellation of our debt of sin is because he died (Heb. 9:26-28).

His blood on the altar shows the fulfilment of the covenant (Heb. 13:20). A covenant or testament is of no value until the testator is dead (Heb. 9:16-22). Christ *died* that the inheritance *might* be ours, and Christ *lives* at God's right hand to guarantee that the inheritance *shall* truly be ours.

3. His blood atonement gives acceptance to our persons and worship

See Ephesians 1:6-7.

His blood removes even the sin of our worship, prayers and works (Isa. 64:6).

His blood enables us to come into the holiest (Heb. 10:19).

Every prayer, act of worship and praise, work of faith and labour of love will be acceptable to God in proportion as it is done or offered through the blood of Christ.

Questions
1. How are God's mercy and God's wrath equally magnified in the shedding of Christ's blood?
2. What does it mean to say, 'The death of Christ is not the cause of God's love but the result of it'?
3. In what way can Christ be called 'the perfect sacrifice'?

16. The ram of consecration

Leviticus 8:22-24

In this chapter Aaron, the high priest, and his sons were consecrated for the priesthood and the service of God about the tabernacle.

vv. 4-5. All that was done this day was according to the commandment of the Lord. It is a picture of all believers who are separated, sanctified, justified and consecrated to the Lord (Rev. 1:5-6).

v. 6. Moses washed Aaron and his sons with pure water, to show that all who bear the name of God and the vessels of God and hold the mystery of faith do so with a pure conscience, clean life and holy motive (1 John 1:5-7),

vv. 7-9. Moses put upon Aaron the coat of fine linen, next to his flesh, the girdle of needlework and the robe of the ephod, which had at its hem the golden bells and pomegranates (Exod. 28:31-35). He then put upon him the ephod made of gold, blue, purple, scarlet and fine-twined linen, which had two shoulder-pieces (Exod. 28:6-12). He put the breastplate upon him, which was made of the same material as the ephod and put upon him the Urim and Thummim, which, according to Exodus 28:17-21, seems to be the twelve stones with the names of the twelve tribes. Then the mitre of fine linen, with the plate of gold declaring, 'Holiness to the Lord', was placed on Aaron's head (Exod. 28:36-38).

vv. 10-12. Moses took the anointing oil and anointed the tabernacle, all that was in it, and Aaron himself, sanctifying them, setting all apart for holy use and service.

In verse 2 the Lord had instructed Moses to take the oil with which he anointed Aaron, a bullock for a sin-offering and two rams — one for a burnt-offering and the other to be a ram of consecration.

vv. 14-17. Moses slew the bullock, putting the blood on the horns of the altar and pouring the blood at the base of the altar, thereby separating it for holy use that it might be fit to have sacrifices offered upon it (Heb. 9:22). But the body of the bullock was taken outside the camp to be burned. This is a picture of our Lord Jesus, God's Lamb, who suffered outside the gates of Jerusalem a painful and shameful death, and the wrath of God was poured out upon him in order to make an atonement for his people (Exod. 29:14). This bullock is a sin-offering.

vv. 18-21. The first ram was slain as a burnt-offering, its blood sprinkled upon the altar. Its body was not taken outside to be burned; it was burned there upon the altar (Exod. 29:18) as a sweet savour or a sweet-smelling fragrance to God. This clearly denotes the delight and pleasure which the Father has in the death of his Son for sinners (Eph. 5:2).

vv. 22-24. The second ram was brought forth and is called 'the ram of consecration' (Exod. 29:22). Let us see three things that are evident.

1. The transfer of the sinner's sins to the sacrifice

In one sense the transfer of our sins to Christ was effected by God through the same eternal covenant and purpose by which the sacrifice was selected (Heb. 7:22; 13:20).

In another sense, the transfer of our sins to Christ was complete when he died on the cross (2 Cor. 5:21; 1 Peter 2:24).

Yet there is also a sense in which the transfer of our sins to Christ becomes a fact in time when we receive Christ as our Lord and Saviour, when we by faith actually lay our hands on Christ and there confess our sins, leaving them with him to bear away. This is what

is demonstrated in verses 14, 18 and 22, when Aaron and his sons
laid their hands upon the heads of the bullock and the two rams.

2. *The death of the bullock and the rams*

Verses 15, 19 and 23 declare that the sacrifices were killed. On
whomsoever the guilt is found, on him must the penalty lie; and from
him must that penalty be exacted to the uttermost. Our sins were laid
on Christ and he must die.

Power is not enough. Even love armed with power is faced with
righteousness, and righteousness is stronger than power.
Omnipotence cannot conquer holiness (Rom. 3:26).

Holiness is not enough. He that would save us must also bow to
the law's last sentence. 'The soul that sinneth shall surely die.'

3. *The consecration of the servants*

vv. 23-24. Aaron and his sons were not plunged into the blood, for
the quantity of blood is of no consequence. The blood was applied
to three places on their bodies, and by this the whole man was
consecrated.

The tip of the right *ear* denotes that his ears were turned only to
the Word of God. 'Speak, Lord, thy servant heareth.'

The thumb of the right *hand* indicates that all of the servant's
skill, talent, resources and effort are dedicated to his master. 'Lord,
what wilt thou have me to do?'

The great toe of the right *foot* signifies that the servant's walk is
changed, consecrated and determined by the blood of Christ. His
walk is in paths of righteousness.

> O Master, let me walk with thee,
> In lowly paths of service free.
> In peace that only Christ can give,
> With thee, O Master, let me live.

Questions
1. What would be the original purpose of the ritual and symbolism
in this process of consecration?

2. Why does the blood of Christ, symbolically applied to a believer, affect every aspect of his life, walk and conversation?
3. How can all three 'senses' of the transfer of the sinner's sins to Christ be said to be an act of God?

17. The Day of Atonement

Leviticus 16:1-22

Before Adam sinned he lived in communion with God, but after he had broken the commandment, he could have no more familiar fellowship with God. Even under the Mosaic dispensation, when God was pleased to dwell among a chosen people, it was painfully revealed that the sin and separation were still there (Isa. 59:2). The presence of God was hidden away from mortal eye, hand and foot. God's presence was revealed in the Holy of Holies of the wilderness tabernacle, and no man might come near except in one way, and then only the high priest once a year — and not without the blood (Heb. 9:1-8).

How can a son of Adam approach God? How can a sinner come before God, be accepted and forgiven? Only in the way God has decreed — no other way! God has, in grace and mercy, purposed to show mercy and grace to sinners in a way consistent with his righteousness, justice and truth. That way is by the obedience and death of his only begotten Son, by whom we have received the atonement (John 14:6; Rom. 5:8-11; Heb. 9:11-12; 10:19-22). Long before Christ came to earth and fulfilled all that was promised and prophesied of him, God pictured the person and work of Christ, our great High Priest and Redeemer, in the Day of Atonement, taught in this chapter.

This Day of Atonement was only a type, a shadow of good things to come by Christ. These sacrifices could not put away sin (Heb. 10:1-4). These blood atonements only continued until Christ died, and they are no more (Heb. 10:11-14,18).

v. 2. The Holy of Holies might be called God's presence-chamber, where he appeared in his glory upon the mercy-seat. Neither Aaron, the high priest, nor any man might approach God except at the time God designated and in the way God appointed.

v. 3. Only Aaron was to come into the holiest place. There were other priests who ministered about the tabernacle, but Aaron represented our Lord Jesus Christ, the one great High Priest of the eternal covenant. All believers are kings and priests unto God (1 Peter 2:9; Rev. 1:6; 5:9-10). But only Christ is the great High Priest, the one mediator, and his atonement and intercession make our presence acceptable.

v. 4. Aaron, the humble and spotless high priest, came into the holiest place. Over and over Aaron must wash his flesh in pure water (Exod. 30:18-21) and be clothed in simple, white linen. Christ, our High Priest, was holy and harmless and undefiled (Heb. 7:26) and having laid aside his glorious adornment, he was clothed in the humility of flesh.

vv. 5-8. Aaron was to select two goats for a sin-offering and one ram for a burnt-offering. The ram was to be offered as an atonement or sacrifice for himself and for his house. He was then to cast lots upon the two goats. One would be for the sin-offering on the mercy-seat and the other would serve as the scapegoat (vv. 20-22). Christ Jesus is both our scapegoat, on whom God laid our sins, and our sin-offering, who died for us.

vv. 12-13. In the first part of the tabernacle there was a candlestick, which represents the light of the world, a table of shewbread, which represents Christ the bread of life and, before the veil, an altar of incense which burned continually. This incense symbolizes the prayers and intercessions of Christ our Lord. When Aaron came into the holiest, he was to bring a censer of live coals and a handful of that incense which he put upon the fire. The cloud of the incense covered the mercy-seat, as the intercession of Christ fills the throne of grace for us (Rom. 8:34).

vv. 14-16. Aaron sprinkled the mercy-seat with the blood of the sin-offering and made atonement for the sins of the people. Our Lord

Jesus has died, entered the presence of God with his own blood and made an eternal reconciliation and atonement for our sins (Heb. 9:11-15, 22-28; 10:12-14).

v. 17. No man was to be anywhere near to Aaron as he accomplished this work of atonement. In just the same way, Christ, our Lord, by himself purged our sins (Heb. 1:3; John 16:32).

The sacrifice of our Lord Jesus enables us to enter into the presence of the eternal, holy God (Heb. 10:19-22). The veil was rent in two when he died (Matt. 27:50-51).

Questions
1. Look at Proverbs 14:12. Why is it essential only to approach God in the way that he has decreed?
2. How does Christ's work as scapegoat and sin-offering so effectively deal with our sin?
3. What does 'atonement' mean?

18. Caleb — the 'faithful dog'

Numbers 14:1-25

This book is about Old Testament pictures of Christ, and while Caleb is not what one would call a type of Christ, yet the story of Caleb's faithfulness to the Lord gives us an excellent text from which to preach Christ and his faithfulness to those who believe him.

The children of Israel encamped below Mt Sinai for about a year and during this time God gave them law, tabernacle, feast days, etc. Moving across the desert with the cloud before them, they came to Kadesh-Barnea (Num. 32:8), on the edge of the desert and on the border of the land God had promised them. The Lord ordered Moses to send men to search out the land which he had given to them (Num. 13:1-20). The spies were in the land for forty days and returned, bringing fruits from the land and their report about the land and its inhabitants (Num. 13:23-29).

All of the spies except two, Joshua and Caleb, discouraged the people from entering the land (Num. 13:31-33). Caleb and Joshua believed God; they urged the people to obey God and go into Canaan (Num. 13:30; 14:6-9).

The people would not hear these two faithful men but rather listened to the majority and would have stoned God's true servants (Num. 14:10). God turned them back to die in the wilderness. All who were over twenty years of age (except Joshua and Caleb) would never enter the land (Num. 14:24,28-33). It is significant to note that Caleb belonged to, and represented, the tribe of Judah, from which our faithful Redeemer came (Gen. 49:10).

1. The name Caleb means 'dog' or 'faithful dog'

I don't know why Caleb's father gave him a name which means 'faithful dog'; a dog is a dog! But I do find that the people to whom the Lord Jesus has been merciful and to whom he has revealed his person and work are never too proud to take unto themselves the name 'dog'. Mephibosheth called himself 'a dead dog' before the mercies of David (2 Sam. 9:8). The Canaanite woman acknowledged that she was a dog before the Lord (Matt. 15:25-27).

Christ came not to call the righteous, the good and the moral; he came to save sinners. He died for the ungodly (Rom. 5:6-8; Matt. 9:10-13). A person must be lost to be saved; he must be emptied before he is filled; he must be humbled before he is exalted. God will put us in the dust of nothingness in order that Christ may have all of the glory (1 Cor. 1:26-31). God will shut our mouths before he opens our ears to hear the good news of redemption in Christ (Rom. 3:19-24).

Men in the Scriptures who were blessed to see the glory of God in Christ confessed themselves to be nothing before him, even that they were dogs! (Job 42:5-6; Isa. 6:1-5; 1 Cor. 3:18).

2. What is it to follow the Lord fully?

Caleb, the faithful dog, was said to have 'followed [the Lord] fully' (Num. 14:24; 32:12; Deut. 1:36; Josh. 14:9). What does this mean?

It is to follow *him*: 'My sheep hear my voice, ... and they follow me.' 'A stranger they will not follow' (John 10:27,5). He is their Lord and Master, and their *only* Master. They delight to do his will: 'Thy will be done.'

It is to *follow* him. They do not run ahead of the Lord, but rather they follow him. They do not move until the cloud moves. We dare not run ahead of his good providence, but are content to 'wait on the Lord'.

It is to follow the Lord *in heart*. 'My son, give me thine heart.' Following the Lord is not a physical exercise, but a heart relationship and experience. Paul declared, 'It is the love of Christ for me and my love for him that constrains me, motivates me and thrills me.' There are many churches with crosses on their steeples which have long since taken the cross out of the pulpit. Our Lord said to Peter, 'If you love me, feed my sheep.' If we love him, we shall! And our obedience, service and labour are motivated by love, not fear nor covetousness.

It is to follow the Lord *all the days of our lives* (Josh. 14:6-14). Caleb was forty years old when he stood firmly before Israel and urged them to believe God and take the land. Forty-five years later he declared, 'I still believe God; give me my inheritance.' Some follow Christ for loaves and fishes, some for miracles and some for tradition and custom. These soon fall away, but those who know, believe and love him will follow him all the days of their lives (Col. 1:21-23; Heb. 3:6,14).

It is to follow Christ *even if we stand alone* (Num. 14:10). Even when all the congregation refused to believe and would have stoned Caleb, he believed God. One man may turn the tide; but turn or not, the man who believes Christ will believe him even if he must stand alone (Acts 20:22-24). Stephen stood alone and died for the gospel he believed.

It is to follow Christ *by the power and strength of his Spirit.* **'My servant Caleb ... had another spirit with him'** (Num. 14:24). It is not by our wisdom that we believe, nor by our merit that we receive grace, nor by our power that we stand. It is by his Holy Spirit. 'Not by might, nor by power, by my Spirit, saith the Lord.' We are made willing in the day of his power, and we are kept by his power through faith. 'Not unto us, O Lord, but unto thy name give glory!' The true believer does not take credit for anything he is, has or does (1 Cor. 4:7; 15:10).

Questions

1. Why must we be cautious of presenting Christ to unbelievers for their 'joy, peace and prosperity'?
2. Christ's sheep will hear and will follow the Lord. Why do they believe, hear and follow when others do not? (See John 10:26).
3. If following Christ becomes hard, what confidence do we have that Christ will not fail us in difficulty?

19. The high priest intercedes

Numbers 16:41-50

The authority of Moses and Aaron had been questioned by Korah, Dathan, Abiram and 250 men of renown in the congregation of Israel (vv. 1-4). Moses tried to show them the unreasonableness of their rebellion (vv. 5-11). Moses commanded them all to appear before the Lord the next day, with Aaron, to have the matter settled (vv. 16-18). When God would destroy the whole congregation, Moses and Aaron interceded for them (vv. 19-22). God opened the earth and swallowed up Korah, Dathan, Abiram, their families and all that pertained to them (vv. 26-33). He then sent fire from heaven and consumed the 250 men who followed them and offered incense (vv. 34-35). The rebellion was not only against Moses (the prophet and leader) but against God's appointed high priest, Aaron (vv. 9-11), which reveals rebellion against God's way of redemption through Christ; for Aaron represents Christ, our High Priest (Lev. 16:17-18,33-34; Heb. 9:7-8).

One would think that this incident would have a lasting effect on the people of Israel, but it did not; for the very next day all of the congregation murmured against Moses and Aaron saying, **'Ye have killed the people of the Lord'** (v. 41). This reveals the total blindness and hardness of the human heart. No amount of signs, miracles, nor witnesses will bring men to God apart from divine regeneration and revelation. In John 5:32-40, our Lord declared to the people who trusted in their religion, 'John bore witness to me, the works I do reveal who I am, the Father himself has verified my claims, the Scriptures testify of me — but you will not come to me!'

The wrath of God arose against the rebellious people and he said to Moses, **'Get you up from among this congregation, that I may consume them'** (v. 45). Moses instructed Aaron to take a censer, put fire in it from off the altar with incense, and go quickly unto the congregation and make an atonement for them before the Lord. The plague from God had begun (v. 46). Aaron, the high priest, ran with the censer of incense and stood between the fallen dead and the living, for the plague had already killed 14,700 people. As Aaron stood between the holy God and the people with the atonement, the plague stopped (vv. 47-49). This is one of the strong Old Testament pictures of our great High Priest, Jesus Christ. We shall consider the type as we look at Aaron.

1. Aaron loved the sinful people

These people certainly did not love Aaron. The whole plot was against him — to strip him of his office and take it unto themselves. Is not this the attitude of Adam's race against Christ? In the Garden of Eden, at the Tower of Babel, and at the cross the cry has been and still is, 'We will not have him reign over us.' 'They hated me without a cause.' We would rob him of all his pre-eminence.

Yet Aaron loved the people, and with no regard for his own life or safety, he rushed down among the people who were under the wrath of God and was identified with them. Christ, our Lord, loved us, came to earth, identified with us in the flesh under the law of God, and took upon himself the form of a servant (Phil. 2:6-8). 'Herein is love, not that we loved God but that he loved us, and sent his Son to be the propitiation for our sins' (1 John 4:10).

2. Aaron acted as God's high priest

Aaron did not rush before God empty-handed with only a plea for mercy and a prayer for compassion. The people had sinned, and the wrath of God cannot be lifted without a sin-offering and an atonement (Heb. 9:22). Aaron brought the censer of incense. So also, Christ, our Lord, as our High Priest, must have something to offer (Heb. 8:1-3). His tabernacle is his body; his sacrifice is himself; his atonement is his own blood (Heb. 9:11-12).

Aaron did not plead their works and deeds, nor promise that they would do better in the future. He held up the atonement. Christ does not plead our righteousness, but his! He does not plead our works, but his!

3. Aaron served as the mediator

The people were dropping like dust as Aaron stepped between them and God to plead God's mercy for them. He was in effect saying, 'Death and judgement, you must march over me and my atonement; you must smite God's high priest and ignore God's atonement if you destroy the people.' Wrath and judgement have a claim on us. Justice is ready to smite the sheep. But Christ, the Mediator, stands between us and the justice of God and says, 'You must walk over me and ignore my blood to destroy my sheep' (1 Tim. 2:5; Rom. 8:33-34).

Aaron, and his atonement, was the only hope the people had, as Christ in you is the hope of glory. Aaron was the unaided mediator: he stood alone waving the censer, as Christ, by himself, purged our sins. Aaron was the sufficient saviour. Death came to his feet and stopped. Even so, our Lord Jesus Christ is the effectual, sufficient Redeemer of all who believe. Judgement must stop at his feet (Rom. 8:1); for 'He is able ... to save them to the uttermost who come unto God by him, seeing he ever liveth to make intercession for them' (Heb. 7:25; 10:12-17).

Questions
1. Christ's love for his people is no weak, sentimental benevolence; it is a power for action and achievement. How may we know that God loves us? See Romans 5:8.
2. God's wrath is justly vented against sin and sinners. How does our great High Priest save us, yet uphold justice?
3. Can another saviour be found among mankind? List some of those that are tried.

20. The brazen serpent

Numbers 21:4-9; John 3:14-18

There is no better type or picture of Christ, our Redeemer, and the way that sinners are saved to be found in the Old Testament than the one before us, for our Lord himself chose this Old Testament picture to illustrate the gospel to Nicodemus, the religious Pharisee (John 3:14-18). Would you learn the way of mercy and life? Then follow this story prayerfully and carefully.

1. The people rebelled against God

vv. 4-5. They were discouraged because of the way. It was away from Canaan instead of towards Canaan, but it was the way they had chosen at Kadesh-Barnea. They could and should have entered the land of milk and honey, but their unbelief turned them away from God (Heb. 3:19).

Our wanderings in the wilderness are of our own choosing. In our father, Adam, we chose not to believe God (Rom. 5:12). We wanted to be our own god and to have our own way, and the consequence was death for the whole race.

The people spoke against God. Paul, in 1 Corinthians 10:9, said they spoke against Christ. They murmured against Moses, God's prophet and leader. Nothing that the Lord or Moses, his servant, had done pleased them. They spoke against the way of God and the Word of God.

Our generation is no different. Instead of recognizing that our condition and troubles in the spirit and the flesh are of our own making and justifying God in his judgements, we murmur against the Lord, his way, his Word and his servants. The lust for our own way (Isa. 53:6; 55:8) got us in the mess we are in, yet we still reject God's way and desire our own.

The people found fault with the bread from heaven (manna) and the water from the rock. **'Our soul loatheth this light bread.'** What a horrible condemning statement, especially in the light of the fact that 'That rock was Christ,' and the manna a picture of Christ, God's gift of life!

How many in the world of religion today are content with Christ, the bread of life and the water of life? (John 5:40; 6:51-52, 55-60). Like Israel of old and the Jews of apostolic days, we will not have this man reign over us nor rejoice in his way of life.

2. The Lord sent fiery serpents among the people

vv. 6-7.   Because of their sin of murmuring and rebellion, God judged the people and sent deadly poisonous serpents among them, and those who were bitten by the serpents died.

Our sin has separated us from our God. The serpent of sin has left its poison in every son of Adam and death, the wages of sin, is upon us (Rom. 5:17-19). 'In Adam all die.'

There was no human cure for the fiery serpents' bite, as there is no human cure for the guilt and condemnation of sin. Spiritual death is in us, physical death is upon us and eternal death awaits us. 'Sin, when it is finished, bringeth forth death.'

The people entreated Moses to intercede for them with God. Only the great mercy of God could deliver them. Grace is God *giving* us what we *do not* deserve, and mercy is God *not giving* us what we *do* deserve.

3. God provided the remedy — a picture of Christ, our Redeemer

vv. 8-9. A serpent was made in the likeness of the fiery serpents. So Christ, our Lord, was made in the likeness of flesh (Rom. 8:3; Phil. 2:7). He was made of a woman, bone of our bone and flesh of our flesh (Luke 24:39). He was numbered with the transgressors (Isa. 53:12).

The serpent of brass had no venom, as Christ had no sin. He was tempted as we are, yet without sin.

The serpent of brass was lifted up on a pole. So Christ was lifted up on a cross (John 3:14-15). Bearing our sins, he was nailed to a cross (Isa. 53:4-6; 1 Peter 3:18).

There was only one remedy — the serpent on the pole. There is only one Saviour, one Redeemer, one deliverer — the Lord Jesus Christ, our substitute (John 14:6; Acts 4:12; John 3:35-36).

All that the people were required to do was look. God provided the remedy fully and completely and commanded them to look. Our command is the same: 'Look and live' (1 John 5:11-13; Rom. 3:28). The remedy was sufficient and effectual for dying sinners. No matter how severe the case, it was 'Look and live'.

The common notion is that salvation is for good people, church workers and those who are examples and moral specimens. But how different is the Word of God and how different this example! God's grace is for the guilty; Christ the Saviour is for sinners (Rom. 5:6-8; Matt. 9:10-13). God's mercy is for the miserable who cannot help themselves. We have no gospel for sham sinners nor pretended professors. Our gospel is for the lost, as Moses' serpent was for the hopelessly bitten Israelites.

An interesting commentary on human nature is found in 2 Kings 18:1-4. The people saved the serpent of brass and began to worship it; so Hezekiah, King of Judah, had to destroy it, calling it 'only a piece of brass'. Do not people today tend to worship the land where Christ lived, calling it the Holy Land? Do they not worship the place where he died and lay buried? Is not the cross itself an object of worship? What idolatry! It is not the cross that saves, but the Christ of the cross.

Questions

1. In what sense might it be said that men sin because they are sinners, rather than that they are sinners because they sin? What is the root problem?

2. What is our condition before God if we 'receive no more than we deserve'? What is mercy?

3. How has Christ reconciled the justice of God and the mercy of God?

21. A Prophet like Moses

Deuteronomy 18:18-22; John 4:25-26

1. It is the clear teaching of the Word of God that our Lord Jesus Christ has a threefold office — Prophet, Priest and King. While others, as types of Christ, have held one (or maybe two) of these offices, no one has ever been prophet, priest and king except Christ.

How good and gracious is the Lord to send among us so great a prophet as 'the Son of God, Emmanuel, God with us'! (Matt. 1:23; 17:5).

What a prophet he is — coming from heaven, above all, having the Spirit without measure, fulfilling what others only talked about, declaring the whole counsel of God and bringing life and immortality to light through his gospel! (John 3:31-35; 2 Tim. 1:8-10).

We see the absolute necessity of such a prophet, without whom we would sit in darkness and be left to stumble in blindness (2 Cor. 4:3-6). But his words are true and faithful, and to hear him is to hear God (John 12:48-50; Heb. 1:1-2).

How blessed are those who hear and believe him (John 5:24), and how inexcusable will be those who refuse to hear him (John 3:18), for he is the one great *Prophet*, of whom Moses was but a type (Heb. 3:3-6). He is the one great eternal *High Priest*, of whom Aaron was but a type (Heb. 7:21-25). He is the one great *King of kings*, of whom David was but a type (Luke 1:30-33).

2. The promise declares that **'The Lord thy God will raise up'** this one great Prophet (Deut. 18:18). All of the true prophets and faithful priests were ordained and sent of God, for no man takes these offices

on himself (Heb. 5:4-5). But this promise is of one person — one prophet who is the Messiah and is actually the Word of God himself (John 1:1-4,14). He that has seen him has seen the Father (John 14:9), and he that has heard him has heard the Father (John 3:33-36).

The promise declares that God would raise up this Prophet **'from the midst of thee, of thy brethren'**. He is of Israel, according to the flesh, of the tribe of Judah and the household of David (Rom. 1:1-3; 9:4-5; Matt. 1:1). He was 'like unto Moses' in that he was a man, he was God's prophet, he was a mediator between God and the people, he performed great miracles and he delivered his people from bondage. But he is infinitely superior to Moses and to all the other prophets, for he is the Son of God! (Heb. 3:1-6; 1:8).

God declares, **'I ... will put my words in his mouth'** (v. 18; John 7:16; 8:28; 17:6-8). His words are the words of *life* — not just true facts concerning God and the kingdom of heaven; he speaks and men live spiritually (John 5:21,24; James 1:18; 1 Peter 1:23), even as he spoke and Lazarus came forth. His words are the words of *truth* (John 1:14,17; 14:6; 18:37). His words are the words of *grace*. He is full of grace and truth. His words bring peace, pardon, life and salvation from sin. That Prophet came not to condemn the world, for the world stood condemned; but he came that we might have life more abundantly. He is the gospel (the good news), and he came bringing the gospel. If any man hears his words and believes on him, he will never die (John 8:51; 14:23-24). The gospel is actually 'the power of God unto salvation' (Rom. 1:16). One cannot separate the Saviour and his Word, for he is the Word. No one can call on him who does not believe him, and no one can believe him who has not heard him (John 5:24; 20:31).

3. There is also a promise given to those who refuse to hear that Prophet — the promise of judgement! (v.19). All who will not hearken to the gospel spoken by Christ, in the name of the Father who sent him, will feel the wrath and judgement of God. To despise the words of Christ is to despise Christ, and to despise Christ is to deny and despise the Father. There is no remedy for rebellion against the Redeemer (John 3:35-36).

We may also note the following points:

1. All other prophets were inspired by Christ and sent by Christ. He is more than a prophet; he is 'God with us' (Matt. 1:23).

2. All other prophets pointed to Christ and spoke of Christ (Acts 10:43). Christ is the sum and substance of their prophecies. He fulfilled and completed all that they foretold (John 1:45; Col. 2:9-10).

3. All other prophets began the holy books and the message of grace. Christ finished and completed the books, the message and the work (Heb. 1:1-3).

4. All other prophets spoke of God by inspiration and learning, but Christ spoke of the Father as being with him and by him (Prov. 8:29-30; John 1:18; Matt. 11:27).

5. All other prophets have left their work and are gone. Jesus Christ abides in all his offices continually. As he is a Priest for ever, so he is the Prophet and the King!

Questions

1. A prophet declares the Word of God. How has Christ perfectly fulfilled this function? Compare John 1:1.
2. Why might we say that Christ *is* the gospel?
3. What are those who reject the gospel effectively doing?

22. The cities of refuge

Deuteronomy 19:1-10; Joshua 20:1-6

The Lord gave to Israel clear instructions for dealing with thieves, criminals and murderers: 'Eye for eye, tooth for tooth, hand for hand, foot for foot' (Exod. 21:24). The Scripture teaches that the punishment shall be according to the crime! If a person murders another in anger and malice, the murderer shall be put to death by proper authority. In many cases this would be by the near kinsman of the victim, called the avenger of blood (Deut. 19:6,12).

However, suppose that two men go into the woods to cut wood and while one is swinging his axe, the head of the axe comes off the handle and strikes his neighbour in the head, killing him. What is to be done? The killer had no hatred, no intention to kill and no malice aforethought.

The Lord instructed Israel to appoint six cities of refuge among the forty-eight cities given to the Levites (three at the beginning and another three as their borders were enlarged). The person who killed another accidentally and unwittingly could flee to one of these cities and state his case to the elders of that city. The elders were to take him in, give him a place to dwell among them, and when the avenger of blood came looking for him, they were not to deliver him into his hands. The slayer could abide in safety until his case was heard or until the death of the high priest (Joshua 20:6). But if the slayer were to leave the city of refuge and the avenger of blood found him and killed him, the avenger would not be guilty (Num. 35:26-28).

The word 'refuge' in the Hebrew means hope, or safe habitation, and is commonly used to denote a place or a person to which or to whom we flee that we may be safe and secure from danger or death.

'The eternal God [in Christ] is thy refuge' (Deut. 33:27). Christ is
the refuge for guilty sinners (Ps. 62:6-8; Heb. 6:18).

> Other refuge have I none;
> Hangs my helpless soul on thee.
> Leave, ah, leave me not alone:
> Still support and comfort me.
> Hide me, O my Saviour, hide,
> Till the storm of life is past;
> Safe into the haven guide,
> Oh, receive my soul at last!

(C. Wesley)

There are so many ways in which these cities of refuge are a type
of Christ, our refuge.

1. The cities of refuge were appointed by God. By God's decree,
will and word these cities provided for the safety and security of
those who fled to them.

It is by God's appointment and divine will that Jesus Christ, his
well-beloved and only begotten Son, became our surety (Heb. 7:22),
our High Priest (Heb. 5:5), our righteousness (Jer. 23:5-6), our
Redeemer (Gal. 4:4-5) and our Saviour (John 3:16-17).

*2. The cities of refuge were to be located so that someone could flee
to a refuge without difficulty.* They were to be easy to find, with signs
pointing along the way, and the highway to these cities was to be
kept clear of obstructions.

Christ, our refuge, is not far from any of us (Acts 17:24-28; Rom.
10:6-10). The guilty have but to look and believe. The Word of God
is the clear sign which points us to Christ (Rom. 10:17; John 5:24).
The preachers of the gospel are to keep the way clear of stumbling-
blocks and obstructions by preaching Christ (1 Cor. 1:17; 2 Cor.
11:3-4).

3. The man-slayer was to flee immediately to the city of refuge. To
delay was foolish. In just the same way, those who would find refuge
from the curse and condemnation of the law must run to Christ *now*
(2 Cor. 6:2).

4. The man-slayer must be within the city to be safe. Knowing about the city or standing near to the city was not enough to be saved; he must be in the city. Those who would find refuge in Christ must by faith dwell in Christ (John 15:5-6; Eph. 1:6). To know about Christ, to profess to know Christ, or even to admire Christ is not to be saved. Believers, like the man-slayer of old, leave all behind and gladly lie in the bosom of the Redeemer, casting all their cares upon him and resting in his sufficient grace (1 Cor. 1:30).

5. The man-slayer must remain in the city. To leave meant death (Num. 35:26-27). Believers will and must continue in faith (Col. 1:21-23). To deny Christ or to depart from Christ is to perish (Heb. 10:38-39).

6. Those who got into the city of refuge before the avenger of blood overtook them were completely safe and delivered from death (Josh. 20:9). All who come to God by the righteousness, blood and mediation of the Lord Jesus Christ, before death and wrath overtake them, are for ever saved and freed from all condemnation (Rom. 8:1; John 5:24).

7. There are ways in which the type breaks down as a picture of Christ.

There were *six* cities of refuge. There is only *one* Redeemer (John 14:6).

These cities protected only from *physical* death. Our Lord Jesus delivers us from *spiritual* death and *eternal* death.

These cities required *physical exertion* and running to reach them. No physical move, effort, nor deed is necessary to come to Christ — only *heart faith*: '*Look* unto me and be ye saved.'

These cities were only for those who *by accident or chance* killed someone; but Christ, our Lord, is the refuge and Redeemer of *wilful* murderers, adulterers, thieves and the chief of sinners. He died for the ungodly and welcomes all sinners to come to him for refuge.

Questions
1. Who needs refuge?
2. What might be said of those in need of refuge who nevertheless refuse it?
3. What is Christ's response to all who flee to him for refuge?

23. Joshua

Deuteronomy 34:1-12; Joshua 1:1-9

The subject matter of the book of Joshua is how Joshua, by divine commission, took upon himself the government of the children of Israel after the death of Moses. In the whole affair, Joshua is a type of the Lord Jesus.

1. His name was Joshua — called in the New Testament Jesus (Acts 7:45; Heb. 4:8). His name, given by Moses, Jehoshua (Num. 13:16), means 'salvation'. Joshua is said to mean 'Jah' (short for Jehovah), 'his help'. Moses received word from God, after the incident involving the striking of the rock (Num. 20:12), that he would not bring the congregation into the land of promise. That responsibility would fall upon Joshua. It is clear that Moses (whose very name is synonymous with the law) could never bring Israel into Canaan, any more than the law can bring us to heaven (John 1:17). This is the work of Joshua (Jesus), our Saviour. Much importance is given to the name of our Redeemer, for his name indicates his character, his work and his glory (Matt. 1:21; Acts 4:12; Rom. 10:13; Phil. 2:9-11).

2. Joshua was for a time the servant of Moses. He was under Moses, obeyed Moses and did the will of Moses, as a good servant. Christ, our Lord, for a time was made of a woman, made under the law (Gal. 4:4). He took upon himself the form of a servant and became obedient in all things as our representative (Phil. 2:6-8; Rom. 5:19). Christ was subject to the law (both moral and ceremonial) in order that he might impute unto his people a perfect standing before the law (Heb. 2:16-18; 4:14-15).

3. Joshua was the governor and commander of Israel. Vested with complete power and authority from God, he led Israel to victory and possession of the land. Our Lord Jesus is King of kings and Lord of lords. He has all authority in heaven and earth (Matt. 28:18), he has all power over all flesh (John 17:2), and he must reign until he has the full salvation of all of his elect (1 Cor. 15:24-28).

4. Joshua led Israel into Canaan, not into sight of it, but into it. So Christ effectually redeems all his people and will take them to glory (John 6:37-39; 10:14-16,27-30). What the law could not do, being weak through the flesh, Christ, our Joshua, has done (Rom. 8:3). Our inheritance is secured by and in Christ (1 Peter 1:3-5).

5. Joshua was a mighty conqueror. He overcame and destroyed many kings and mighty men so that Israel could have peaceable possession of the land of Canaan. So our mighty conquerer, the Lord Jesus, overcame and totally destroyed the mighty rulers and enemies of our souls (Eph. 6:12). He defeated Satan, the king of evil. He conquered sin, which, like a tyrant, rules over the sons of men. He conquered death, the king of terrors (1 Cor. 3:21-23).

6. All of the good promises to Israel were fulfilled at the hands of Joshua. So all the gracious promises of God to his elect are fulfilled in and by the Lord Jesus.

> What he has promised, he is able to perform (Rom. 4:21).
> He is able to subdue all things unto himself (Phil 3:21).
> He is able to keep that which we have committed to him (2 Tim. 1:12).
> He is able to save to the uttermost them that come to God by him (Heb. 7:25).
> He is able to keep us from falling and to present us faultless before the presence of his glory (Jude 24).

7. Joshua was faithful and merciful to save Rahab, the harlot, and her house that had the red cord hung out of the window. So Christ is merciful and faithful to save all sinners who express faith in his blood.

Come, ye sinners, poor and needy,
Weak and wounded, sick and sore;
Jesus, ready, stands to save you,
Full of pity, love and power.
Let not conscience make you linger,
Nor of fitness fondly dream;
All the fitness he requireth
Is to feel your need of him.

Questions

1. The law is strong to condemn and weak to save. Compare this with Christ (see John 3:17).
2. Could the people have entered Canaan without Joshua? May we secure glory without Christ?
3. Why was it necessary for Christ to be a servant of, or subject to, the law?

24. The scarlet line in the window

Joshua 2:1-22; 6:17,23,25

My interest in Rahab, the harlot, and her story is enhanced by the number of times she is mentioned in the Scriptures. Besides the attention given her in the book of Joshua, Matthew identifies her as the wife of Salmon (a prince of the tribe of Judah), mother of Boaz and great-great-grandmother of King David (Matt. 1:5-6). Hebrews lists her in faith's hall of fame along with Abraham, Isaac and Moses (Heb. 11:31). James gives two illustrations of true faith evidenced by obedience — Abraham and Rahab (James 2:20-25).

Israel was camped across Jordan and their commander, Joshua, sent two men to spy the land secretly. They would be taking, especially, the city of Jericho. Jericho was a large city — the one nearest to them and first in importance, for it must be taken. Judging from information that we have, several things are evident. Rahab's house was upon or in the wall which circled the city (Josh. 2:15). Her house was one where a person could find food and lodging. This was why the spies stopped there (Josh. 2:1). It is mentioned several times that she was a harlot. In those times and countries, women who kept public houses and inns were also prostitutes.

Word got to the King of Jericho that these Israelites had been seen at Rahab's house, and the king sent word to her to deliver these men to him. She hid the spies up on the roof of the house and sent word to the king that, although the Israelites had been to her house, they had fled earlier and might be overtaken if the king would send someone after them, which he did. As soon as the king's men left Jericho to pursue after the spies, the gate of the city was closed. Rahab came up on the roof where the spies were hidden and set forth in such a beautiful manner her faith in the living God (Josh. 2:8-11). She then sought the mercy of the Lord to be upon her and her household when the people of God took the city (Josh. 2:12-13). The men promised her that she would be spared provided that she keep faith in not telling anyone of their business (Josh. 2:14), that she hang outside her window this scarlet line by which she let them down the wall, and that she and her family remained inside the house while the battle raged (Josh. 2:18-19). Her house was on the wall with the front facing the city, for the entertainment of persons who came there, and the back was on the outer side of the wall. She let the spies down the wall by the scarlet cord, and they fled in safety to the mountains. When Israel took the city, Joshua commanded that Rahab be spared (Josh. 6:17,22-25).

1. *Rahab is a picture of God's mercy and grace to sinners,* for she was a sinner by birth and by practice. All of the explaining by moralists and legalists will not make Rahab anything but what she was — a notorious sinner. But the Lord Jesus came to save sinners (1 Tim. 1:15; Matt. 9:10-13; Rom. 5:6-8). His mercy is to the miserable and his grace for the guilty.

2. *Rahab is an example of electing, distinguishing and efficacious grace.* It was not by accident that the spies stopped at her house. They were led there by the Spirit of God. Her speech to the spies (Josh. 2:8-11) indicates a heart enlightened and taught by God. Faith is not the product of natural thought and logic; it is the gift of God (Eph. 2:8-9). She was one of the Lord's own and her testimony is proof of her knowledge of the true God, her faith in him, and shows her to be a believer (John 6:44-45).

3. *The scarlet cord she put out of the window was an emblem of the blood of Christ,* by which salvation is accomplished. That scarlet cord which she, by faith, dropped from her window is as decisive and clear a picture of Christ's blood as Abel's lamb, or the Passover blood on the door, or the sin-offering in the tabernacle. It is by his blood and faith in his blood that sinners have redemption, forgiveness, atonement, safety and protection from the avenging justice and wrath of God. 'When I see the blood, I will pass over you.' When they saw the scarlet cord in the harlot's window, they passed by her house and destroyed all others.

4. Rahab and her family were told to come into her house where the scarlet cord was hung and *there only would they be safe*. As the Israelites were told to stay in their houses, where the Passover blood was sprinkled, so Rahab and her family were to remain under the protection and safety of the blood of Christ. To venture outside was to be destroyed (Josh. 2:18-19).

Under the blood of Jesus,
Safe in the shepherd's fold;
Under the blood of Jesus,
Safe while the ages roll;
Safe though the worlds may crumble,
Safe though the stars grow dim;
Under the blood of Jesus,
I am secure in him.

Questions
1. 'Electing, distinguishing and efficacious grace.' What does this phrase mean?
2. What is the importance of the shedding of blood in the work of redemption?
3. Rahab's hope of deliverance was the red cord and the promise. What is the foundation of a believer's hope?

25. The birth of Samson

Judges 13:1-25

The preacher of the gospel of Christ will find many things about Samson that will enable him to illustrate the person and work of Christ Jesus.

1. Samson's birth was miraculous, his mother being barren. God sent him.
2. Samson's birth was foretold by an angel of the Lord.
3. Samson was sanctified from the womb — he was a Nazarite.
4. Samson was a mighty man who destroyed the enemy and delivered Israel.

A whole chapter in God's Word is given to the appearance of the angel of the Lord to Samson's mother and father, and in this chapter we find some strong assurance and confidence in our Samson, the Lord Jesus Christ.

v. 1. **'The children of Israel did evil ... in the sight of the Lord.'** This evil was idolatry, a sin to which they were prone and of which they were frequently guilty. God delivered them into the hand of the Philistines for forty years as punishment for their idolatry.

vv. 2-5. The angel of the Lord appeared unto the wife of Manoah, of the tribe of Dan. She was barren and had never conceived. He told her that she would bear a special son, who would be a Nazarite from the womb and would mightily deliver Israel out of the hand of the Philistines.

A Nazarite was a man or woman who, under Hebrew law, bound himself or herself to abstain from wine and all products of the grape, to wear long, uncut hair and to observe various forms of purification in the service of the Lord. The period of observance of the vow varied, but could cover a lifetime. When the period was concluded, offerings were made, the hair was cut and burned and the Nazarite was discharged from his vow (Num. 6:1-21). Paul assisted four Christian Jews in this ceremony (Acts 21:20-26).

vv. 6-8. The woman came and told her husband all that she had seen and heard, and Manoah prayed unto the Lord that he would again send the messenger of God and further instruct them concerning the child.

vv. 9-14. The angel of the Lord appeared again unto them. We have no doubt that this was the Lord Jesus Christ himself, who often appeared in human form to saints in Old Testament times (Gen. 14:18; 32:30; Judg. 6:22-24). Verses 18 and 22 indicate that this angel of the Lord was Christ. His name is 'secret' or wonderful (Isa. 9:6). Other angels did not hesitate to identify themselves (Luke 1:19; Dan. 10:13).

vv. 15-22. Manoah asked the man of God to allow him to offer a lamb before him, but he declined saying, 'If you would offer a burnt offering, offer it to the Lord.' Manoah did not know that this was the angel of the Lord, though his countenance was unusual (v. 6); so he would have been honouring the creature rather than the Creator (v. 17). So Manoah offered a kid upon a rock unto the Lord, and as the flame and smoke arose, the man or angel of the Lord ascended to heaven in the flame. Manoah and his wife fell on their faces, realizing that this man was indeed the angel of the Lord! Manoah said to his wife, 'We shall surely die, because we have seen God' (Exod. 33:20). His faith wavered in the presence of such miracles and majesty.

v. 23. But Manoah's wife was strong in faith and wisdom, and she encouraged him with a threefold argument. May we, as believers in the grace and mercy of God in Christ Jesus, be encouraged by the same arguments.

1. 'If the Lord intended to destroy us, *he would not have received the burnt offering.*' They were commanded by the Lord to offer a burnt offering, which they did, and the Lord was pleased to show his approval and acceptance by ascending in the very flame of the sacrifice.

Our Lamb has been sacrificed on Calvary. By faith we look to Christ, the Lamb of God. 'For God was in Christ, reconciling the world unto himself' (2 Cor. 5:19). It cannot be that Christ loved the church and died for it and the church should die also. It cannot be that the Lord laid our iniquity on him and on us also. The Lord Jesus is himself our sacrifice and has not only died but risen and ascended to God's right hand (Heb. 1:3). This is our assurance of grace and mercy.

2. 'If the Lord intended to destroy us, *he would not have showed us all these things.*' He showed himself in two appearances. He showed his acceptance of the sacrifice by identifying himself with it.

Our Lord has revealed himself to the sons of Adam in the person of the Lord Jesus (John 10:30; 14:9). Our Lord has revealed his justice, holiness and righteousness in the sacrifice of his own dear Son (Rom. 3:25-26). Our Lord has showed us the way of life in the obedience and death of Christ. If he did not purpose to save a people, why would he reveal to them Christ, the way of life? (John 14:6).

3. 'If the Lord intended to destroy us, *would he have told us such wonderful things as these?*' The word to them was that they would have a son called Samson, who would indeed deliver the people from bondage.

This is the foundation of our faith — to believe God! (Rom. 4:19-25). When we are depressed or filled with doubt and fear, let us go to the Word, the promises of God, and believe! Believe not your feelings nor your human reason, but believe God! God has told us the Saviour would come; he has come! The Old Testament says, 'Someone is coming'; the New Testament says, 'Someone has come and will come again' (Isa. 7:14; 9:6; John 4:25-26).

88   *With New Testament eyes*

Questions
1. The Lord Jesus Christ's death has been accepted by God in substitutionary payment for sin. Can God demand payment for sin twice?
2. For whom was Christ a substitute? For whom did he die?
3. The Lord has revealed himself as the only way of salvation. Why has he done this? (See Matt. 1:21).

26. The kinsman redeemer

Ruth 1-4

A young minister was told by an elder of a Welsh chapel that he had preached a very poor sermon because Christ was not in his sermon. The young man replied, 'Christ was not in the text.' The wise old man said, 'Christ is in every text. In every text of Scripture there is a road which leads to Jesus Christ and him crucified. Your business is to find that road and get on it.'

All that most people know about the book of Ruth is what Ruth said to Naomi in Ruth 1:16-17, and they usually come away from that with high thoughts of Ruth and no thoughts of Christ. The real key to the book of Ruth is in the term 'kinsman' found in Ruth 2:20; 3:9,12; 4:14. The 'kinsman' is the one who has the right to redeem (Lev. 25:25).

Because of a famine in the land, a man called Elimelech, of Bethlehem-Judah, sold all that he had and, with his wife and two sons, left the land of Israel and moved to pagan Moab. Elimelech died in Moab and his two sons married Moabite women, lived with them ten years, and then they both died. Naomi, now a very poor widow, determined to return to Judah and told her two daughters-in-law to remain in Moab with their people and their gods. Orpah kissed Naomi and departed, but Ruth clave unto her and uttered those blessed words found in Ruth 1:16-17.

1. Here is a picture of ruin by the Fall

1:19-21. When Naomi, now old, poor and weary, came to Bethlehem, the people gathered about her and exclaimed, **'Is this**

Naomi?' Is this the same Naomi who left Bethlehem a few years ago, rich and prosperous with her family about her? She replied, **'Call me not Naomi** [sweet and pleasant]; **call me Mara** [bitter], **for the Almighty hath dealt very bitterly with me.'** She went out full and came back empty, went out rich and came back poor, went out sweet and came back bitter.

We look at Adam after the Fall, when he sinned, sold out and left the presence of God for his own way, and we say, 'Is this Adam? Are these poor, dying, corrupted creatures sons of Adam, created in the image of God?' (Rom. 5:12; 3:10-19). The king is now a beggar, the prince is now a pauper and the blessed are now cursed.

2. *Here is the unmerited, unsought love of Christ for sinners*

2:1-5,16. Naomi and Ruth came to Bethlehem in the beginning of the barley harvest season. It was the custom to allow poor people and those without support to follow the reapers in the field and pick up what they had left. Ruth went out to glean in the fields, and by God's providence she gleaned in the field of Boaz, Naomi's near kinsman (2:1,3). Boaz took notice of Ruth, had compassion on her, instructed her to glean in his field and told the reapers to let fall some **'handfuls of purpose'** (2:16) for her.

This world belongs to the Lord Jesus. It is his by design, by decree and by death (Col. 1:16-17; John 3:35; Rom. 14:9; John 17:2). We live and glean in his field. The Lord Jesus in grace and love has taken notice of some of Adam's race. He knew us though we knew him not; he loved us though we did not love him, and by his handfuls of purpose, we have lived and prospered to this day. God takes care of his own even in their days of unbelief.

3. *Here is the Kinsman Redeemer*

2:18-20. Ruth returned home with a generous supply of grain. Naomi took note of the abundance and asked Ruth where she gleaned and who was so generous with her. When Naomi heard that Ruth's benefactor was Boaz, she exclaimed, **'Blessed be he of the Lord, who hath not left off his kindness.'** Boaz is one who has the right to redeem, a kinsman-redeemer. If someone has sold his inheritance and has a near kinsman, who is able and willing to stand for him and buy back all that he lost, it shall be done (Lev. 25:25).

Christ Jesus, by God's covenant of mercy and divine grace, is our Kinsman; for he became a man, numbered with the transgressors, bone of our bone and flesh of our flesh (John 1:14; Gal. 4:4-5). He willingly took upon himself to redeem all that we lost in Adam, and he is able to do so because, though a man, he is the strong and mighty God (Heb. 7:25; 2 Tim. 1:12; Jude 24-25). By his perfect obedience he has given us righteousness before the law, and by his death he has satisfied divine justice, enabling God to be both just and justifier of all who believe (Rom. 3:25-26).

4. Humility, acceptance and redemption

Read in Ruth 3:1-7 how Ruth humbled herself at the feet of Boaz, seeking his mercy, as we lie at the feet of Christ, for he owes us nothing. Read in Ruth 3:10-11 how Boaz accepted her whom he already loved, even as we are accepted in the Beloved upon evidence of humility and faith. Read how Boaz married Ruth and all of his wealth and his name became hers, even as we are married to Christ and are joint-heirs with him because we are his and wear his name. The pagan girl became the wife of Boaz, the great-grandmother of King David and stood in the lineage of Christ — all of grace!

Questions
1. As sons of Adam, all men are poor, dying and corrupt before God. Why is this?
2. Though helpless, we have a kinsman, able and willing to help. Yet why should he?
3. We may trace every blessing a believer possesses to the unconditional love of God for his people. Can we enquire beyond this?

27. The song of Hannah

1 Samuel 2:1-10

A godly man named Elkanah had two wives. One was named Hannah and the other was named Peninnah. Hannah was much loved by her husband, but the Lord had shut up her womb and she had no children. Peninnah had several children and, being jealous of Hannah, continually provoked and harassed her because she was barren. Peninnah was especially unkind to Hannah when their husband was away, so that Hannah wept and would not eat.

The next time Elkanah went to Shiloh to worship and sacrifice unto the Lord, he took Hannah with him. Hannah was in much distress of soul, and she wept and prayed before the Lord that he would give her a son (1 Sam. 1:9-11). She promised to give this son unto the Lord all the days of his life. Eli, the priest, saw Hannah praying and weeping, but because no words came from her mouth, he thought she might be drunk, so he reprimanded her (1 Sam. 1:12-14). Hannah explained her sorrow and her desire to the man of God, who prophesied that God would grant her request (1 Sam. 1:15-18).

Hannah and Elkanah returned home and a son, Samuel, was born to them (1 Sam. 1:19-20). The men of a household were required to appear before the Lord at the three festivals; the women were not. Therefore, when Elkanah and his household went up to offer unto the Lord, Hannah would not go, for she said, 'I gave him to the Lord to serve before the Lord, so I will not take him until he is old enough to remain there and not return home with me' (1 Sam. 1:21-23). According to reports, there was a threefold weaning of a child in old times: the first when he was weaned from the mother's milk at two or three; the second when he was weaned from a nurse at seven; and the third when he was twelve and weaned from childish manners. So Samuel was about twelve years old when Hannah took him up to Eli (1 Sam. 1:24-28).

Hannah had prayed for a son, and God heard her prayer. Then, as she fulfilled her vow and brought him before the Lord, she gave thanks and magnified the Lord. 'Oh that men would praise the Lord for his goodness, and for his wonderful works to the children of men!' (Ps. 107:8).

v. 1. **'My heart rejoiceth in the Lord'** — not in my husband, my son, nor even in my happiness and fulfilment, but *in the Lord* (Phil. 3:3). The Lord Jesus is the fountain of grace and the giver of all (James 1:17-18).

'My horn [strength] **is exalted in the Lord.'** The change in her state and her strength to conceive was by his power and grace (Col. 2:13). Spiritual life is in and by Christ (John 1:12-13; 5:21).

'I rejoice in thy salvation.' When she spoke of her enemies, Hannah probably referred to those who mocked her in her barrenness. But, judging from verse 10, she also had a wider meaning, for Christ is God's King and his anointed, and it is through Christ that we have the victory over our enemies, Satan, sin, death, hell and the grave (1 Cor. 15:25-26).

v. 2. **'There is none holy as the Lord.'** Here is a well-taught believer who understands that God's chief attribute is his holiness. God is essentially, originally, perfectly and unchangeably holy, as others are not!

'There is none beside thee,' holy, righteous and just. All that God does is in accordance with, and in keeping with, his holiness. Christ came, lived, died and arose that God may be holy, just and the justifier of sinners (Rom. 3:25-26).

'Neither is there any rock like our God.' Our Lord Jesus is often called the Rock. He is our Rock and our salvation, to hide, shelter and support all who come to him (Ps. 62:6-7; Isa. 28:16; 1 Cor. 10:4).

v. 3. **'Talk no more so exceeding proudly.'** We have no room to complain if we are barren and no room to boast if we are blessed (1 Cor. 4:7; John 3:27). Arrogant words and thoughts will be judged, for God knows every heart (Dan. 5:20; James 4:6). Actions are weighed before God by the motive and principle from which they proceed.

vv. 4-5. Hannah, praising God's grace to the humble and weak, illustrates how he exalts the humble and resists the proud. Mighty men, trusting in their strength and arms, are broken to pieces, while God gives strength to those who stumble in weakness. Those who have proudly lived in plenty are forced to toil for bread, while the hungry have been filled by his grace. Barren Hannah, by his mercy, has borne several children, while proud Peninnah (according to tradition) can bear no more and loses those she has (Jer. 9:23-24). God's grace is a gift to the needy and humble, not a reward for the rich (Matt. 5:3-7).

vv. 6-7. It is true that the Lord sovereignly, according to his purpose, controls all things, and men live and die, succeed or fail, are rich or poor and rule or serve by the will of God. But it is also true that before God saves a sinner and reveals Christ to his heart, he will strip that sinner of all self-righteousness, all self-hope and all personal merit. God will bring us low before he exalts us, strip us before he clothes us, and show us our poverty before he reveals our inheritance in Christ (Matt. 9:10-13; Phil. 3:4-10).

v. 8. Here is a description of our state in sin — poor beggars in the dust and on the dunghill (Eph. 2:12-13). But, because of our Lord's righteous obedience and shed blood, we are seated with him among princes on the throne of glory (Eph. 2:4-10).

vv. 9-10. His word and his covenant will not fail. He will keep his saints, his sheep, and not one of them will perish (John 6:37-39; 10:27-30). He will judge the wicked, and none can stay his hand. The Lord will give power, strength and victory to his King, the Messiah (John 17:23; Ps. 24). Christ came to set the captive free and he will not be discouraged (Isa. 61:1-3).

Questions

1. What is providence?
2. As our 'actions are weighed before God by the motive and

principle from which they proceed', what is the value of rules and regulations of conduct?

3. Out of spiritual barrenness comes life and fruitfulness. Who, and what, is the source of our spiritual life?

28. 'Give us a king'

1 Samuel 8:1-22

Samuel, Hannah's son (whose name means 'asked of God'), remained with Eli, the priest and prophet of God, and ministered unto the Lord before Eli (1 Sam. 2:11; 3:1). Eli was quite old and had failed to discipline his sons; therefore, God slew them (1 Sam. 3:10-14). Samuel became God's prophet and judge in Israel (1 Sam. 3:19-21). Samuel was a faithful prophet of God all the days of his life (1 Sam. 7:15-17). When he was old, Samuel made his sons judges over Israel but, like Eli's sons, they perverted judgement, took bribes and displeased the Lord (1 Sam. 8:1-3). The elders of Israel came to Samuel and requested that he establish a king over Israel, like the nations around them (1 Sam. 8:4-5).

This matter had arisen before, during the days of Gideon (Judg. 8:22-23); and Gideon had wisely replied to their request, 'I will not rule over you, neither shall my son rule over you; the Lord shall rule over you.' The people of God have no king but Jesus Christ, the Lord (Matt. 23:8-11). Christ is King of kings and Lord of lords (Acts 2:36; Rom. 10:9-10; Phil. 2:9-11).

The request of the elders displeased Samuel, and he knew it to be evil. But he took the matter to the Lord in prayer, and the Lord revealed what was really behind their request. **'They have not rejected thee,** [Samuel], **but they have rejected me, that I should not reign over them'** (1 Sam. 8:6-8).

Thomas, the disciple, summed up the faith and submission of all believers when he said, 'My Lord and my God.' Christ is our King by the Father's design and decree; he is our King by his death (he died that he might be Lord of the dead and the living); and he is our King by our submission. It is his crown-rights that men refuse to own. 'We will not have this man to reign over us' (John 19:15). He was delivered to Pilate, charged with saying, 'He himself is Christ a King' (Luke 23:1-2). The soldiers mocked him as 'King of the Jews' (John 19:1-3). Over his head, nailed to the cross, was the charge against him: 'Jesus of Nazareth, the King of the Jews' (John 19:19). And it is as Prophet, Priest and King that believers recognize, receive and bow to the Lord Jesus, not just as 'personal Saviour'. There are those in modern religion who talk of accepting Jesus as their Saviour but not as their Lord. This is an impossibility! One knows nothing of the saving mercy and merits of Christ who does not bow to Christ, the Lord! Israel was glad to receive God's blessings, but not his reign! They never refused his benefits, but they refused his sceptre! One noted evangelist often said, 'Christ will be Lord of all, or not Lord at all.' Christ said to his disciples, 'Ye call me Master and Lord: and ye say well; for so I am' (John 13:13). Redemption is the enthronement of Christ in the heart. A man cannot serve two Masters. Our Lord demands of those who would be his disciples total submission and surrender to his lordship (Matt. 10:34-39).

The Lord told Samuel to tell the people what to expect when they rejected his reign and made a man to be king over them (1 Sam. 8:9-18). But the blind and foolish people only cried out the more, **'Nay; but we will have a king over us'** (1 Sam. 8:19-20). Samuel heard their words and rehearsed them in the ears of the Lord; and the Lord said, **'Make them a king'** (1 Sam. 8:21-22; 10:18-19).

The first order of business of the new king, Saul, after he had reigned only two years, was to usurp the authority of the priest, reject God's way of atonement and offer a sacrifice himself to God (1 Sam. 13:1,8-14). The people reject Christ the King and then Christ the Priest and sacrifice.

Questions

1. Samuel was rejected by the people, but in reality, they were rejecting God himself. What might this teach us about a believer's witness among unbelievers?
2. Can we receive Christ as Saviour without accepting him as Lord?
3. What does it mean to acknowledge Christ's kingship and bow before his sovereign authority?

29. Saul's great sin

1 Samuel 13:1-14

vv. 1-2. Saul had reigned for one full year over Israel and was near the end of his second year when he chose 3,000 men of Israel for constant military service and protection. 2,000 were with him and 1,000 were with Jonathan, his son. The rest of the men returned to their homes to be summoned if needed.

vv. 3-4. Evidently the Philistines had garrisons and strongholds in the land, and Saul ordered Jonathan to surprise and destroy the garrison of the Philistines near Geba. There must have been some sort of agreement or understanding between Israel and the Philistines, for we are told that, because of this treacherous attack, 'All Israel did stink with the Philistines,' as men void of honesty and trust. Jonathan did it on orders from his father, the king. Knowing that the Philistines would retaliate, Saul sent messengers to call all the people to prepare for war, for his defence and theirs.

vv. 5-7. The Philistines gathered together a great and mighty army, **'as the sand ... on the seashore in multitude,'** to fight against Israel. When the people heard of the slaughter of the Philistine garrison, of the anger of the Philistines over it and the war plans of the enemy, they knew that they and their new king were in deep trouble. Many of them began to hide in caves, rocks, mountains and pits. Some of them fled across Jordan to the land of Gilead, as far as they could from danger. Those who stayed with Saul in Gilgal **'followed him trembling'** and afraid. Saul had not sought the counsel of God's prophet nor the will of God in any of these matters; all of this trouble was of his own making.

v. 8. When Samuel first anointed Saul (1 Sam. 10:8), he ordered him to tarry seven days in Gilgal, promising that at the end of those seven days, he would come to him, offer sacrifices and tell him what God would have him do. Perhaps this was a general rule to be observed at Gilgal on all occasions, for Saul was waiting for Samuel as the people scattered from him.

v. 9. Wait on the Lord, wait for the prophet of God to speak for God (Heb. 1:1), and wait for the prophet-priest to offer the Lord's sacrifice. This order Saul broke. He offered the burnt offering. Though he was neither prophet nor priest, because he was a king, he thought he could do anything. Uzziah paid dearly for this presumption (2 Chron. 26:16-21). There is no area where the judgement of God is more severe and the wrath of God more certain than when any man presumes to violate the sin-offering, sacrifice and atonement, for this is the work of Jesus Christ alone (Heb. 1:3). All through the Scriptures men have perished who have sought to approach God apart from the priest and the true blood offering which typifies Christ, our great and only High Priest.

Men who tampered with God's revealed way of acceptance and communion have felt the hand of judgement, for this is a denial of our sin and a disregard for his holiness. Examples are Cain (Gen. 4:3-5); Nadab and Abihu (Num. 3:4); Moses (Num. 20:9-11) and Uzzah (2 Sam. 6:6-7).

Among all of Saul's rebellions and blunders, this was his greatest error and chief offence — to come before God without the appointed priest and true sacrifice (Heb. 5:1-5; 8:8-12; 10:11-14). To attempt to come to God apart from his ordained priest and sacrifice is to deny our sins and to deny God's holiness, righteousness and judgement against us (Rom. 3:19-26).

v. 10. When Samuel did come, Saul seemed to boast of what he had done rather than to repent of it, and he went out to bless Samuel, as if he thought himself a complete priest empowered to bless as well as sacrifice. This is the pride of the human heart. Only Christ can save, sanctify and bless (Col. 2:9-10; 1 Cor. 1:30).

vv. 11-12. When Samuel asked Saul what he had done, he began to justify his actions.

    1. 'I was losing the support of the people, for they were leaving.'
    2. 'You did not come when we thought you would.'
    3. 'The armies of the enemy were gathered together.'
    4. 'The enemy planned to attack us, and I had not entreated the blessings of God, so I forced myself to offer a sacrifice.'

He failed to realize that no circumstances, no cause and no situation can warrant a violation of the sacrifice of Christ and his priesthood. 'No man cometh to the Father but by me' (John 14:6).

vv. 13-14. Saul had acted foolishly and proudly in acting as God's priest and offering a sacrifice. Not only had he broken God's commandment regarding the sacrifice, but he had acted as his own saviour and mediator, denying the absolute necessity of the person and work of the Lord Jesus Christ (1 Tim. 2:5). The anointed, ordained priest, offering the designated sin-offering and sacrifice before God, at the time and in the way God appointed, is a picture and a type of the Lord Jesus Christ, our great High Priest, and his atonement. Any deliberate violation of this sacrifice is a rejection and denial of Christ. This was Saul's sin, and God took the kingdom from him and raised up David, a man after his own heart.

Questions
1. Saul displayed little concept of the holiness and righteousness of God. What of those who today presume to come to God apart from Jesus Christ?
2. What does this teach us about the religions of this world, be they ever so sincere?
3. Many professing Christians use the right words, attend the right places and act out acceptable practices. After all, was Saul so far out in his worship of God?

30. David and Mephibosheth

2 Samuel 9:1-13

Saul, the people's king, had been rejected by God for disobedience and rebellion (1 Sam. 15:26), and David, a man after God's own heart (1 Sam. 13:14), now reigned over all Israel. One of David's first acts as king was to enquire of the house of Saul, **'Is there yet any that is left of the house of Saul, that I may show him kindness for Jonathan's sake?'** Ziba, a former servant of the house of Saul, reported to David that Mephibosheth, son of Jonathan, was still alive and was a cripple, lame on both feet. David sent and fetched Mephibosheth and gave him the estate of Saul, with many servants and a place at the king's table all the days of his life.

This is a beautiful picture of the grace and mercy of God towards unworthy sinners for Christ's sake, which can be told in seven words.

1. **'And the king said'** (v. 3). Where the word of the king is, there is power, authority and total sovereignty. There is no council, no conference and no bargaining here. The king speaks from his throne of authority, and what he decrees shall be done.

Our God is infinitely sovereign over all his *creation*. He reigns in total authority in heaven and earth (Ps. 115:1-3; Dan. 4:34-35).

Our God is sovereign in *providence* (1 Sam. 2:6-8; Isa. 45:5-7; 46:9-11). There may be second and third causes, but God is the first cause of all things (Rom. 8:28; Eph. 1:11).

Our God is sovereign in *salvation* (Exod. 33:18-19; Rom. 9:15-18; Jonah 2:9).

2. **'That I may show the *kindness* of God to him'** (v. 3). The word 'kindness' is 'mercy'. David, the king, was a man of mercy. The house of Saul were David's enemies and deserved no mercy nor pity, but David found it in his heart to show mercy to some.

Our God is holy, righteous and just, but he is also merciful. He delights to show mercy (Ps. 130:3-7). Adam's race is a fallen, rebellious race and deserves no mercy. God is not indebted to sinners, but he has determined to show mercy to some (Exod. 33:18-19). The language of religion is merit, rewards and service, but the language of true redemption is mercy. 'I obtained mercy' (1 Tim. 1:13-16). 'God be merciful to me a sinner' (Luke 18:13).

3. **'Which is *lame* on his feet'** (v. 3). Ziba, the servant of the house of Saul, reported to David that Jonathan had a son called Mephibosheth, who lived in Lo-debar and who was now a poor cripple because of a tragic fall when he was young (2 Sam. 4:4).

The word 'lame', through a fall, not only describes Mephibosheth, but it is our condition since the fall of our father, Adam (Rom. 5:12,17-19; 1 Cor. 15:21-22; Eph. 2:1-3). All of our faculties were affected by this fall, and in our flesh there dwells no good (Rom. 3:9-19).

4. **'Then King David sent, and *fetched* him'** (v. 5). King David purposed to show mercy to someone of Saul's house. When he heard that Jonathan had a crippled son in Lo-debar, David sent his servant to where Mephibosheth was and fetched him; that is, the servant called and brought him to David.

The Lord of glory is love, and love must be expressed. The Lord of glory, in his sovereign mercy, determined to show mercy to a fallen race. He set his love and affection on lame sinners and sent his only begotten Son into the world to be our Saviour (John 3:16-17; Gal. 4:4-5; Rom. 5:6-10). Christ came where we were, became what we are, and by his obedience and death honoured the law, satisfied justice and enabled God to be just and justifier of all who believe (Rom. 3:19-26; 1 Peter 3:18). He then sent his Holy Spirit to fetch us, call us and make us willing to come to him (Gal. 1:15; Eph. 1:13-14; Ps. 110:3).

5. **'And David said ...** *Fear* **not'** (v. 7). Mephibosheth was afraid in the presence of the king because he was of the house of the king's enemy; therefore, he fell on his face before the king and did reverence. David said, 'You have no cause to be afraid; I will show you kindness.'

Men and women who know something of God's holiness, their own nature and sin, and what the law and justice of the king demand, have every reason to be afraid in his presence. God will punish sin. 'The soul that sinneth, it shall surely die.' 'The beginning of wisdom is the fear of the Lord' (Ezek: 18:20; Ps. 111:10; cf. Luke 18:13).

6. **'I will surely show thee kindness** *for* **Jonathan thy father's** *sake*' (v. 7). David said, 'I have not fetched you to destroy you; so you need not be afraid. I will surely (certainly) show you mercy for the sake of Jonathan, your father, whom I love.' Before Mephibosheth was born, David had made a covenant with Jonathan, promising to show mercy to Jonathan's sons because of his love for him (1 Sam. 20:11-17).

Before the foundation of the world, God the Father entered into an everlasting covenant of mercy with the Lord Jesus Christ, giving him a people out of Adam's race and making Christ the surety and Redeemer of those people (John 6:37-45; 10:24-30; 17:1-3,9; Eph. 1:3-14; 2 Thess. 2:13; Heb. 13:20-21). The mercy and kindness God shows to sinners is because of his love for Christ (Rom. 8:35-39). It is for Christ's sake (Col. 1:14-18).

7. **'For he did eat** *continually* **at the king's table'** (v. 13). David fulfilled every promise to Mephibosheth, as God will fulfil every promise to his elect in Christ, for none will ever perish, but all will be made like Christ and enjoy his presence for ever (Rom. 8:33-39).

Questions
1. Why is it essential that we receive mercy and reject all idea of merit?
2. What does 'total depravity' mean?
3. At best Mephibosheth might have been ignored, at worst, put to death at the mere word of the king. How does the actual outcome teach us about the nature of God's mercy?

31. Why God permitted David to fall

2 Samuel 11,12

Two chapters of the Word of God are given to the great sin of David in taking the wife of Uriah the Hittite and having her husband murdered. Preachers often refer to this sin of David and rightfully condemn it, but few enquire into the reasons why God permitted David to fall when he could easily have prevented it, as he constantly hedges all believers about and keeps them from the Evil One and from great sin.

1. The first thing to acknowledge in David's rise and fall, in his victories and defeats, in his spiritual success and failure, is *the sovereign hand of God*. The hand of God, our Father, is never removed from his child, and God is the first cause of all things (whether he directs it or permits it) for his glory and our good (Rom. 8:28-31). Satan could not attack Job without God's permission (Job 1:8-12). Joseph's brothers had no power to sell Joseph into slavery without God's permission (Gen. 45:5-8). Paul's thorn in the flesh, called 'the messenger of Satan', was ordained of God (2 Cor. 12:7).

2. All the experiences of God's people in the Scriptures, both good and bad, are *for our instruction and example* (1 Cor. 10:1-13). The Word of God is not like the flowery biographies of men. God's Word does not conceal the bad and reveal only the good of his saints. Men are portrayed exactly as they are — sinners saved and kept only by the grace of God. As we read the Word of God, we are taken directly into the most intimate and personal lives of men like Noah, Abraham, Lot, Aaron and Simon Peter. Some of God's choice

people are seen in very poor character. Some are permitted to sin greatly before meeting Christ, like Saul of Tarsus, and some are permitted to sin greatly after meeting Christ, like David and Simon Peter. But none is permitted to continue in sin! (1 John 1:8-10).

3. David's sin clearly sets before us the deceitfulness of the human heart and teaches us to *put no confidence in the flesh* (Jer. 17:9). David's fall came when he was what we call 'a father in Israel'. He had walked with God many years, he had endured many trials, he had won many victories, he had written many psalms and he was a man after God's own heart; yet he fell into great sin. That which is born of the flesh is flesh and will remain flesh until God calls us home. Paul mourned over his fleshly nature and inability to walk perfectly before God (Rom. 7:18-25).

We are foolish to put any confidence in the flesh. Our confidence is only in Christ (Phil 3:3; Ps. 118:8-9). We are often quick to acknowledge a flaw in the character of another and so slow to recognize the potential to sin in ourselves (Matt. 7:1-5; Gal. 6:1-3). Every believer would be wise to recognize and acknowledge that we all partake, stand and continue in the grace of God by his power and not our own. 'I am what I am by the grace of God.' We are 'kept by the power of God through faith' (1 Cor. 15:10; 1 Peter 1:5; 1 Cor. 4:7).

4. David's sin reveals *the grace of God in Christ Jesus* to the chief of sinners (1 Tim. 1:15). David pronounced judgement on himself when Nathan told him the story of the poor man's lamb (2 Sam. 12:1-6). David became angry and declared, **'The man that hath done this thing shall surely die.'** David said in effect, 'This man is a son of death and worthy to die.' Is this not what we are by nature and what we deserve from the hand of God? Nathan replied, **'Thou art the man,'** which caused David to exclaim, **'I have sinned against the Lord.'** Some believe that Psalm 51 was written at this time, confessing his sin and justifying God in condemning him.

'The Lord ... hath put away thy sin' (2 Sam. 12:13). Oh, what good news to the heart of David! He wrote, 'Blessed is he whose transgression is forgiven, whose sin is covered. Blessed is the man unto whom the Lord imputeth not iniquity' (Ps. 32:1-2). Yet sin is not put away nor forgiven because we confess it, acknowledge it and grieve over it. Sin can only be put away by a perfect and sufficient sacrifice. Christ put away our sin by the sacrifice of himself (Heb. 9:26; Eph. 1:7; 1 Peter 1:18-19).

David judged himself, confessed his sin and justified God (Ps. 51:4). But God cannot overlook sin, pass over sin, nor forgive sin apart from the atonement of Christ. He is a 'just God and a Saviour' (Isa. 45:21-22). He must be 'just and justifier' (Rom. 3:25-26). God saves and forgives by Christ, our High Priest, sacrifice and mediator (Heb. 10:12-22).

Questions

1. Many people are willing to acknowledge God's sovereignty in directing nature and organizing the cosmos. Is this a satisfactory view of God's involvement in human affairs?

2. Given vent, the human heart will conceive and enact all manner of evil conduct. Whose responsibility is this?

3. Is there any limitation upon God's willingness to forgive sin through Jesus Christ?

32. Comfort from God's covenant

2 Samuel 23:1-5

There is something special about a man's last words — especially those of a man 'after God's own heart', a man greatly used of God, whose words were often spoken and written under divine inspiration. When a man is dying, I am sure that he must do some serious thinking about three things: his relationship with God, how he will fare in the great judgement and where he will spend eternity. David, in this great hour, found his comfort and hope in God's covenant of mercy and grace. May I find my hope and comfort where he found his!

'**David, the son of Jesse.**' He was a mere man, a mortal like you and me. He was a son, a father, a husband and a friend. Real blood flowed through his veins, and his flesh was as earthbound and as frail as ours (James 5:17).

'**The man who was raised on high.**' David was an object of God's favour and grace. God took a shepherd-boy and made him a king. In our case, he took a beggar from the dunghill and, through Christ, made him to inherit the throne of glory (1 Sam. 2:8; Eph. 2:1-7). Who can tell the great things God has done for us in Christ? (1 Cor. 2:9-10).

'**The anointed of ... God.**' David was anointed King of Israel by Samuel on orders from God, even as we have been made kings and priests (Rev. 5:9-10; 1 John 3:2) by and through the person and work of Christ.

'**The sweet psalmist of Israel.**' David wrote most of the Psalms for Israel and set them to music. They were sweet and delightful to the ear, for they praised and magnified the Lord God.

'**The Spirit of the Lord spake by me.**' The Psalms and songs which he wrote were not the fruits of his own clever tongue and pen, but were written by him under the inspiration of the Holy Spirit (2 Peter 1:21).

'**He that ruleth over men must be just, ruling in the fear of God.**' This character, in all respects, was found in David (2 Sam. 8:15). I believe, though, that David speaks here of Christ, our King of kings and Lord of lords, the Son of David (Isa. 11:1-5; Jer. 23:5-6). He is a just God and a Saviour (Isa. 45:21-22). By his perfect life and death, he enabled God to be just and justifier of all who believe (Rom. 3:25-26). He did not destroy the law, but fulfilled and honoured it. He did not compromise justice, but fully satisfied it (1 Peter 3:18; 2 Cor. 5:21).

'**He shall be as the light of the morning, when the sun riseth.**' No doubt that this is Christ, who is 'the light of the world', 'the sun of righteousness,' who did away with the clouds of law, ceremony and sacrifice and brought in the clear gospel day of full justification, redemption and rest. One writer translates this to read, 'And as the light of the morning shall arise Jehovah the sun.' 'The tender grass' may refer to his incarnation, as in Isaiah 53:2.

'**Although my house be not so with God.**' Here is a great sigh and mournful song. 'All of my house, my children, my servants, my court and my nation are not right with God. They do not love God, worship God, nor seek his glory' (2 Sam. 18:33). David wept over his house and his people, as Paul wept over Israel (Rom. 9:1-3; 10:1).

'**Yet [God] hath made with me an everlasting covenant.**' The covenant by which the kingdom was settled on David and his seed, Jesus Christ, for ever (Luke 1:31-33), is but a type of the eternal covenant of grace, made with Christ from the beginning, in which Christ is surety, saviour, sanctifier and mediator of all given him by the Father (John 6:37-39; 17:2-3; Heb. 13:20-21; 7:22). All that the Father chose, the Son redeems and the Spirit calls (Eph. 1:3-14). What the Lord does, it shall be for ever (Eccles. 3:14) and is without change (Mal. 3:6; Rom. 11:29).

'**Ordained in all things and sure.**' The mercies and grace of God are not left to chance but are decreed, determined and purposed by him (Isa. 46:9-11). The fulfilment of his covenant in establishing a perfect righteousness and effectual atonement is not in the hands of men but given to Christ to accomplish (Gal. 4:4-5; 1 Tim. 1:15);

therefore, they are called the sure mercies of David (Isa. 55:3; Acts 13:34; John 10:14-18,27-30), for he shall not fail nor be discouraged.

'**This is all my salvation.**' It would be good for us to listen to David when he says, 'God's love for me in Christ, God's choice of me in Christ, God's righteousness fulfilled in Christ and God's acceptance of me in Christ is all my salvation' — not my feelings, works, nor righteousness, but his grace (Eph. 2:8-10).

> My God when I approach thy throne
> And all thy glory see,
> This is all my stay and this alone,
> That Jesus died for me.

'**And all my desire.**' Not only do I find comfort and peace in God's covenant of grace in Christ, but I find delight and assurance therein. This is my one great desire — that God's purpose in Christ be fulfilled and Christ have the pre-eminence (Col. 1:18; Phil 2:9-11).

'**Although he make it not to grow.**' At present there are not many signs and evidences of what we are, have or shall be, but the promise is sure and we will rejoice in him (Hab. 3:17-18; 1 John 3:2-3).

Questions

1. In the hour of death, where will you find hope and comfort?
2. Who are the parties to the eternal covenant of grace, and why is this a great source of assurance to the believer?
3. What is the basis of salvation, firstly, for those who are saved by grace, and secondly, for those who are working their ticket to heaven?

33. 'I will not offer to God that which costs me nothing'

2 Samuel 24:10-24

Regardless of the circumstances found in verse 1, a condition which we find hard to explain, David sinned in numbering Israel (v. 10). The Lord gave David a choice of three punishments: seven years of famine, three months of fleeing before his enemies, or three days of pestilence in the land (vv. 12-13). David refused to make a choice but rather said, **'Let us fall now into the hand of the Lord; for his mercies are great; and let me not fall into the hand of man'** (v. 14). The Lord sent a pestilence upon Israel and destroyed 70,000 men (v. 15). When the angel stretched out his hand to destroy Jerusalem, the Lord said, **'It is enough'** (v. 16); and David was commanded to build an altar at the threshingfloor of Araunah, the Jebusite (vv. 18-19).

When Araunah saw David and his servants coming to him, he bowed himself before the king and asked his mission. David said, 'I have come to buy your threshingfloor to build an altar unto the Lord, that the plague may be stopped' (vv. 20-21). Araunah replied, 'Here is the threshingfloor, the wood and the oxen; take them all without charge; they are yours' (vv. 22-23). The king said, 'No! But I will buy it of you at a price; I will not offer burnt offerings unto the Lord of that which costs me nothing.'

A thankful heart will not come to God bearing a gift which costs him nothing. If it is of no value to you, it will not be received nor blessed of God.

When the apostle Paul taught the early church the grace of giving, he referred to the gift of Christ for us — Christ gave himself. 'Though he was rich, yet for your sakes he became poor, that ye through his poverty might be rich' (2 Cor. 8:7-9). This is the reason our Lord commended the widow's gift (Mark 12:41-44). She gave sacrificially, she gave what she needed and was of great value and she gave all she had! Like David, her love for God demanded a gift worthy of him — her all!

Churches and professed Christians today insult God with many of their so-called gifts and efforts to raise money for Christian causes. They give that which costs them nothing. Bakery and candy sales, car washes and jumble sales are held; used clothing, furniture and articles which no one needs are given. Investments are offered which yield a high rate of interest to the buyer. Worthless hillside land is given as a church site. One thing all of these projects have in common is that they cost the giver nothing. There is not in any of them the element of grace, self-denial, nor sacrifice.

Let us look at five lessons learned from David's example.

1. Our example in the Old Testament is that *the first fruits belonged to God:* the firstling of the flock, the choice lamb and the first-born son.

God rebuked the priests of Israel for offering mouldy bread, lame and sick sheep upon the altar. He said, 'Offer these kinds of gifts to your governor and see if it pleases him' (Mal. 1:6-8).

2. *A gift which costs nothing reveals a lack of faith* in Christ, while gifts of true value and sacrifice reveal a genuine faith in the Lord's power to supply our need (Phil. 4:19; Matt. 6:31-33).

Abraham was willing to give his well-beloved son because he believed God (Gen. 22:12). Many in the early church were so strong in faith that they sold their possessions and goods and shared them with poor believers (Acts 2:44-45). No true gift of faith and sacrifice goes unnoticed by our God (Mark 10:28-30).

3. *A gift which costs nothing reveals a lack of love* for Christ, while true love considers no labour, no cost, no sacrifice too great. 'Jacob served seven years for Rachel; and they seemed unto him but a few days, for the love he had to her' (Gen. 29:20). True love is always liberal and open-hearted, and when love is missing, what men give is considered an investment, a charity, or a loss. 'For God so loved ... he gave his only Son.'

4. *A gift which costs me nothing reveals a lack of regard for the majesty and glory of God.* Dare I offer anything to the Lord of glory which is less than my best? The quality and value of our gifts depend largely on the esteem and respect we have for the recipient.

If you were selected to provide a gift for the head of state and one for the paper-boy, would there be more thought and sacrifice in one than in the other? A gift given in the name of God demands our best.

5. *A cheap, part-time, and selfish course of religion, which costs nothing, is an abomination to God and will never be accepted.* The man who found one pearl of great price sold all that he had and bought it (Matt. 13:45-46). Christ said, 'If any man will come after me, let him deny himself, and take up his cross, and follow me' (Matt. 16:24-26).

Read about Elijah's instructions to the widow who only had enough ingredients for one cake of bread. 'Make me a cake first,' he said (1 Kings 17:9-16). She did, and her blessings were multiplied.

Questions
1. 'Church funds should consist of the offering of the gathered believers, not the charity of outsiders.' Is this good economics?
2. Grace is free, but following Christ will be costly. Is this a problem for a believer?
3. What value can be placed on the gift of salvation through the sacrificial death of Jesus Christ?

34. The Queen of Sheba comes to Solomon

1 Kings 10:1-9

It is quite evident that the Queen of Sheba's visit to Solomon is a picture of the sinner coming to Christ, for our Lord himself referred to it in Matthew 12:42: 'The queen of the south shall rise up in the judgement with this generation, and shall condemn it; for she came from the uttermost parts of the earth to hear the wisdom of Solomon; and, behold, a greater than Solomon is here.'

v. 1. The queen **'heard of the fame of Solomon'**. She heard from others of the wisdom of Solomon (1 Kings 3:5-14; 4:29-30). She heard of the wealth and glory of his kingdom (1 Kings 10:6).

Have we not heard of the person and work of Christ? (Gal. 4:4-5; Isa. 7:14; 9:6). Have we not heard of the deity and glory of Christ? (Heb. 1:1-5). Have we not heard of the wisdom and power of Christ? (1 Cor. 1:16-19). Have we not heard of the death and resurrection of Christ? (1 Cor. 15:20-28). As Paul told Festus, 'These things were not done in a corner!' (Acts 26:25-26).

v. 2. The queen, having heard of Solomon, came to him to see and hear for herself. The queen took the right course: she came directly to Solomon.

Is this not the thing for the sinner to do? Come to Christ; come directly to him; do not be satisfied with only hearing of him (Matt. 11:28; John 7:37-39; 6:37-39). Robert Howie was asked by a man, 'Please write down in black-and-white what I am to believe. There are so many texts; give me one to read and believe.' Howie replied, 'It is not any one text, nor any number of texts that save, any more than a man-slayer could be saved by reading the signposts on the road to the city of refuge. He must go to and enter the city. Salvation is in Christ and in coming to him. When a man is thirsty, he is not satisfied by studying the well, but by drinking' (John 6:53-57; Col. 1:27; Gal. 4:19).

The queen came to prove Solomon with many hard questions. She **'communed with him of all that was in her heart'**. She asked questions she could not answer, and others could not answer, but Solomon could.

Christ is the wisdom of God; Christ is the truth. If a man would know God and the mysteries of redemption and life, let him ask of Christ (Luke 10:22; John 1:18) great and hard questions.

1. How can a man be just with God? How can he be clean that is born of woman? (Rom. 3:19-23).
2. How can God be just and justifier (Rom. 3:24-26).
3. How can a man be born when he is old? (John 3:4-8).
4. If a man die, shall he live again? (John 11:25-27).
5. Who can solve the mystery of the Gentiles? (Eph. 2:11-16).
6. How is it that God sees and knows all things, yet he does not see nor remember a believer's sins? (Heb. 10:11-17).
7. All Old Testament prophecies, pictures, types and sacrifices point to someone and to some great event. Who is he? (Luke 24:44-47; Acts 10:43).

v. 3. **'And Solomon told her all her questions,'** for, as a type and picture of our blessed Lord, **'there was not anything hid from the king'** (John 3:34-35).

vv. 4-7. When the queen had seen Solomon's wisdom, the house he had built, his riches and piety, she was quite astonished, like one in ecstasy who had no power to speak because what she saw and heard so affected her. She said to the king, 'What they told me of you was true; actually, the half was not told me. Your wisdom and prosperity exceed anything I thought or heard. It was not until I came and saw that I really believed.'

Though we heard of Christ's love, mercy, grace and glory, it was not until we came to him in faith that we saw and experienced

Christ, the wisdom and power and glory of God (Job 42:1-6; Isa. 6:1-4; 1 John 1:1-4). We stand amazed in the presence of our Lord, realizing that it is impossible to put into words the riches of his grace and glory (2 Cor. 12:2-4).

v. 8. The queen exclaimed, **'Happy are thy men, happy are these thy servants, which stand continually before thee, and that hear thy wisdom.'** We can say with greater emphasis, for a greater than Solomon is here, 'Blessed is the man whom thou choosest' (Ps. 65:4). 'Blessed is he ... whose sin is covered' (Ps. 32:1-2). Blessed are the eyes that see and ears that hear (Matt. 13:16). Blessed is the man whose delight is in the Lord (Ps. 1:1-3). Blessed are those who know him, love him and dwell by faith in him.

v. 9. Then the queen blessed the Lord God, who delighted in Solomon, who put him on the throne of Israel to do judgement and mercy. The Lord loved Israel for ever and made Solomon their king.

The Father loves the Son and has given 'all things' into his hands (John 3:35). The Father delights in the Son and gave him pre-eminence (Prov. 8:23-30; Matt. 3:17). The Father made Christ the surety, Prophet, Priest and King of spiritual Israel because he loved them all in Christ with an everlasting love. Christ came to the earth to honour God's law, satisfy God's justice, to do judgement and justice, that God may be just and justifier of all who believe (Rom. 3:25-26).

Questions
1. How *can* God be just and justifier?
2. What causes can you find for a believer's blessed condition?
3. Why are all the blessings of a believer's life a source of praise to God?

35. Three examples of faith

1 Kings 17:8-16; 18:29-39; 20:31-32

Long ago, when the Roman Empire flourished, someone said, 'All roads lead to Rome.' Those who study the Scriptures with a desire to know the only true God and Jesus Christ, whom he has sent (John 17:1-3), will do well to learn this first: in the Scriptures all roads lead to Christ — his person, glory and redemptive work (Acts 10:43; John 5:39). From Genesis to Malachi the Old Testament Scriptures declare, 'Someone is coming'; the four Gospels declare, 'He has come; behold, the Lamb of God,' and the epistles declare, 'He is coming again.'

I want to consider three examples of faith (recorded in 1 Kings) and how they relate to us: the faith of the *elect*; the faith of the *evangelist* and the faith of the *enemy*.

1. The faith of the elect

1 Kings 17:8-16. Our Lord Jesus referred to this widow in Luke 4:25-26, when he preached in Nazareth and set forth his sovereign power and mercy as the Messiah (Rom. 9:14-18).

God sent a famine upon the land for many years. The word of the Lord came to Elijah, God's prophet, to go eastward and hide by the brook Cherith, and there he would be fed by the ravens and drink of the brook (1 Kings 17:1-4). After a time, because there was no rain, the brook dried up, and the Lord commanded the prophet to go to Zarephath, or Sarepta, a city of Sidon. **'Behold I have commanded a widow woman there to sustain thee'** (v. 9). Elijah found the woman gathering sticks to build a fire. The prophet told her to fetch him a little water in a vessel, and as she went to get the water, he also asked her to **'Bring me ... a morsel of bread.'** The woman replied, 'All I have left is a handful of meal in a barrel and a little oil in a cruse. I am gathering these sticks to build a fire and cook one last cake for me and my son. It will be our last meal, and then we die.' Elijah answered, 'Don't be afraid; go, build the fire and prepare the meal, but make me *a little cake first* and bring it to me; then prepare one for you and your son. For thus saith the Lord, the barrel shall not be empty and the oil shall not cease until God sends rain' (vv. 10-14). The widow did as she was commanded, and the promise of God was fulfilled towards her (vv. 15-16).

How wonderful and sovereign are the ways of our God! He will reject the strength and wisdom of the flesh that he may have all the glory (1 Cor. 1:25-31). In the time of famine, he would send his prophet to a Gentile city, to the poorest of women, a widow, to be fed and cared for.

This woman was one of God's elect, for, though she knew it not, God had already prepared her heart to receive his prophet and his Word. God said, 'I have commanded her' (see Ps. 110:3; Gal. 1:15-16; 2 Thess. 2:13).

The woman heard the words of the prophet and the promise of God to bless and sustain her, and she believed — the evidence of her faith being that she prepared a cake for the prophet first and brought it to him. Like Abraham of old, she believed God against all human reason, logic and hope and staggered not at his promise (Rom. 4:17-25).

The faith of God's elect might be summed up in this way:

Knowledge — 'I know whom I have believed.'
Confidence — 'I am persuaded that he is able to keep.'
Commitment — 'That which I have committed unto him'
(2 Tim. 1:12).

2. *The faith of the evangelist*

1 Kings 18:29-39. In the third year of the great famine, Elijah called the 450 prophets of Baal and the 400 prophets of the groves to Mt Carmel and challenged them to call on their gods, and he would call on the name of the Lord; and the God that answered by fire, let him be God (vv. 19-24). After the false prophets had utterly failed after crying out all day, Elijah's confidence and faith in the living God is seen in two things: first, soaking the sacrifice, wood and altar with twelve barrels of water (vv. 30-35); second, his brief, God-glorifying, prayer (vv. 36-37). '**The fire of the Lord fell.**' 'I believe, Lord, help thou mine unbelief.'

3. The faith of the enemy

1 Kings 20:31-32. Ahab sinned against God in sparing the wicked Ben-hadad, whom God had appointed to destruction, but the faith of these enemies in the mercy of the King of Israel, and the way that they came to him, is certainly a lesson for all guilty sinners who seek the mercy of God. Come in the sackcloth of repentance, with a rope around your neck, justifying God's right to destroy you, and owning your just condemnation (Luke 23:39-43). God is plenteous in mercy to those who seek mercy (Ps. 130:2-8), but the proud he will send away empty. Death, the wages of sin, we have justly earned and deserve, but the gift of God is eternal life through Jesus Christ, our Lord (Rom. 6:23).

Questions
1. How is true repentance manifested?
2. If you have faith, think about your knowledge of Christ, your confidence in his completed work and your commitment to follow him by his grace.
3. Does your faith embolden you to contend for truth in the face of apparently overwhelming opposition?

36. Where is the Lord God of Elijah?

2 Kings 2:1-15

Our story actually begins back in 1 Kings 19:15-21. The Lord revealed to Elijah that he had chosen Elisha to take his place as the prophet of God to Israel.

Every believer is in the Lord's body and has a vital part in the Lord's kingdom and the ministry of the gospel (Rom. 12:4-8). We are all witnesses of Christ. But it is certain that some men are chosen of God to be prophets, apostles, evangelists (missionaries) and pastor-teachers (Eph. 4:11-14). This is not a work or ministry which a man takes upon himself to be a pastor, overseer and preacher of the gospel; but it is a work for which God equips, calls and sends a man (Col. 4:17; 1 Tim. 1:12; 2 Tim. 4:5,11). If God sends a messenger, he will give him the message, the wisdom and the grace needed, and he will give him a hearing (Ezek. 33:30-33).

Although Elijah knew that God had his hand on Elisha and that Elisha would be a prophet of God, he did not pressure the young man nor encourage him to take upon himself such an awesome task and responsibility. He rather discouraged him and put objections and discouragements in his way (1 Kings 19:20). Elijah cast his mantle over Elisha, and when the young man said, 'I will follow thee,' Elijah told him to 'Go home; I have said nothing to you about serving the Lord with me.' Men do not call prophets and preachers; God does! This he said to try him, to get out of his heart what God had done in him. Elijah would not persuade and push this man into the ministry, but rather did all that he could to keep the flesh out of the way and allow the Lord alone to deal with Elisha. But Elisha would not be discouraged and made a feast to express his joy at being called to such a service. He left his employment, his home and parents and his friends and followed God's prophet, became his servant, where he attained knowledge and understanding of divine things and was trained by Elijah (1 Kings 19:21). It seems evident in the Scriptures that the Lord trains his preachers not in schools and seminaries, but under the eye and hand of those who are his preachers and pastors.

vv. 1-8. The time came when the Lord would take Elijah into heaven, and the old prophet was still testing his young servant. He said to Elisha, 'The Lord sent me to Bethel; you stay here.' But Elisha knew his call and replied, **'I will not leave thee.'** Three times Elijah tried to get the young man to leave him, but he would not. Elisha, out of affection for Elijah, aware that God spoke through him, desiring to see and learn all that he could from him and knowing that he needed God's spirit and power, which was upon Elijah, would not leave and enter a work for which he knew he was insufficient, without taking advantage of every moment of this wonderful occasion. Has a man ever learned enough, seen enough, studied enough, or heard enough to feel that he is ready to speak for God? Elisha did not think so! Elijah smote the waters of the Jordan, and they went over on dry land.

vv. 9-15. Before Elijah was taken away into heaven, he asked the young prophet what he desired more than anything else. Elisha did not ask for fame, riches, long life, nor any of the things that appeal to the flesh. He asked for the presence of the Spirit of God. **'I pray, let a double portion of thy Spirit be upon me.'** Elisha did not ask to go with Elijah, but that the presence of God might be with him. Elisha did not grieve over God's providence, but sought the power of God to fulfil his ministry.

When God took Elijah up into heaven, Elisha took up the mantle of Elijah, smote the waters and cried, **'Where is the Lord God of Elijah?'** He was saying, 'O, God, who was with Elijah, be thou also with me.' Men are as nothing; it is the Lord we seek, serve and glorify.

1. The God who blessed and used Elijah must bless and use us.
2. The God who kept Elijah faithful throughout his life on earth must make us stand firm in the faith (Jude 24-25).

3. The God who provided for Elijah in the wilderness must supply our needs (Phil. 4:19).

4. The God who raised the dead by Elijah's word must speak through us to raise dead sinners (Eph. 2:1).

5. The God who gave Elijah courage to face kings and enemies must free us from the fear of men.

6. The God who divided the waters for Elijah to pass over must be with us when we come to that river.

7. The God who took Elijah to glory must take us to himself.

Spirit of the living God, fall afresh on me.
Melt me, mould me, fill me, send me.
Spirit of the living God, fall afresh on me.

Where is the Lord God of Elijah?

1. He is in the heavens (Ps. 115:2-3).
2. He is in Christ (Matt. 1:21-23; 2 Cor. 5:19).
3. He is in his Word (1 Peter 1:23-25).
4. He is on a throne of grace (Heb. 4:16).
5. He is in the midst of those who worship (Matt. 18:20).
6. He is in every act of providence (Rom. 8:28). He is in every breeze, every cloud, every moment, every heartache, every tear and every joy. 'Lo, I am with you always.'
7. He is in all who believe! (John 14:23; 17:23; Col. 1:27).

Questions
1. Qualifications for ministry among God's people are often sought at Bible colleges and the like. Are these God's qualifications? Who equips God's preachers?
2. What is the essential qualification of every preacher of Christ? (See John 14:26).
3. Where is your Lord God?

37. Empty vessels filled

2 Kings 4:1-7

The most essential thing in my life is a knowledge of the Scriptures. The greatest blessing God can bestow upon me is to give me his Word and the grace and wisdom to understand and believe its message of redemption in Christ Jesus (John 5:39; Luke 24:44-45; Acts 10:43).

When you look into a mirror, you see three things. You see the mirror, you see yourself and you see other things that are in the room. When you look by faith into the Word of God, you see three things. You see Christ, who is the Word. You see yourself as you truly are, for the Word reveals the true nature of man. You see others about you and your relationship to them (Isa. 6:5).

In 2 Kings 4:1-7, a godly man had died and left his wife and family in debt and without support. The widow appealed to Elisha for help. He asked her what she had, and she replied, 'Nothing but a pot of oil.' He told her to gather together all the empty vessels she could find, to borrow from neighbours, **'not a few'**, but many empty vessels. Then she was to go into the house, shut the door, and she and her sons were to pour oil from the pot she had into the empty vessels. When all the vessels they had were full, the oil stopped, and she sold the oil and paid her debt.

There are many lessons of grace and mercy in Christ to be learned from this story.

1. The true *character* of a person *cannot be determined by* his *possessions and position in this world*. This man feared and served the Lord, though he lived poor and died poor. If, by God's

providence, we are well off, let us use these means to minister to others (Matt. 25:34-40; James 1:27). If, by God's providence, we are poor, let us trust him to supply our need (Phil. 4:19; Ps. 37:25). The Lord provided for this woman even after the death of her husband.

2. The kind of vessels she was told to bring were *empty vessels* (v. 3). Elisha emphasized that all of the vessels she brought were to be empty — not half-full, not primed with power, nor magic liquid, but empty! This is perhaps the most difficult lesson we who come to God for mercy, grace, salvation and provision have to learn: 'In my hands no price I bring, simply to thy cross I cling.' All who come to Christ must come totally void of merit, works, goodness, or even the beginnings of grace. He makes the dead to live, the blind to see, the lame to walk and clothes the naked (Eph. 2:1-10).

A man once said to C. H. Spurgeon, 'Don't you think the greatest hindrance to salvation is our sinful self?' Spurgeon replied, 'No! I do not! The greatest hindrance to salvation is our righteous self. No man is too bad to come to Christ, but many are too good. He fills the empty, clothes the naked and saves the lost.'

We must learn this first: if someone comes to Christ for his grace, he must come as an empty vessel. It is remarkably plain in the Word of God that Christ passed by the so-called righteous and called sinners, publicans and harlots (Matt. 9:10-13).

3. The number of vessels to be brought were **'not a few'** but *many*! (v. 3). 'Is anything too hard for the Lord?' (Gen. 18:12-14).

He can save *many* sinners. Our Lord commanded us to go into all the world and preach the gospel to every creature, for he is able to save to the uttermost all who come to God by him. Paul wrote, 'Whosoever shall call upon the name of the Lord shall be saved' (Rom. 10:13). These are great and large words.

He is able to save *all kinds* of sinners. The size of the vessel, the age of the vessel, the shape of the vessel and the condition of the vessel were immaterial. It was only to be brought *empty*. This is the command of Christ: 'Come unto me, all ye that labour and are heavy laden, and I will give you rest' (Matt. 11:28).

4. The vessels were *completely filled* (v. 6). The Word is full. From complete ruin to eternal glory our sufficiency is Christ. From

absolute emptiness to the fulness of God, all that we need is met in
Jesus Christ (1 Cor. 1:30; Col. 2:9-10). When an empty sinner by
faith receives Christ, he receives all that God requires, commands
and gives of eternal life (Col. 1:12-13). All spiritual blessings are in,
by and through the Lord Jesus (Eph. 1:3-6). Nothing needs to be, nor
can be added to what Christ is, has done and is doing (Rom. 8:29-
34). 'All the fitness he requireth is to feel your need of him.'

5. When did the oil stop? *When the last empty vessel was full!* As
long as there was an empty vessel in the house, the oil of God flowed
freely and sufficiently, but when the woman called for another
empty vessel and there was none, the oil stopped!

It is so today! As long as there is an empty, needy sinner, the grace
of God flows full and free. Where you have spiritual need, you have
mercy. Where men are lost, Christ saves. Where you have sinners,
you have salvation. The well of mercy never runs dry, and the
cupboard of grace is never bare (Ps. 130:7). But when men are full,
rich, increased with goods and have need of nothing, the oil of grace
stops!

When the last stone of his living temple (Eph 2:19-22) is laid, and
the last empty vessel is filled, the oil of grace will cease and
judgement will fall on the earth. When they were all in the ark, the
door was shut and the rain fell!

> Dear dying Lamb, thy precious blood
> Shall never lose its power,
> Till all the ransomed church of God
> Be saved to sin no more.

Questions
1. What does it mean to be 'empty' as we approach God for
salvation?
2. What is it, in the nature of grace, that demands no contribution
from men and women? (See 1 Cor. 1:27-29; Romans 4:4-5).
3. What does 'the sufficiency of the death of Christ' mean?

38. Naaman, the leper

2 Kings 5:1-14

If we read the story of Naaman, the leper, two questions come forth: could the waters of the Jordan River cure leprosy? The answer is no! Could Naaman be healed of his leprosy without going down into the waters of the Jordan? The answer is no! Then what have we here? The Lord was humbling a proud sinner. The Lord was pleased to show his sovereign mercy to this Gentile sinner (Luke 4:27), but Naaman (like any son of Adam) must be emptied, humbled and brought to understand and acknowledge that salvation and mercy are the gift of God, which is neither deserved nor bought. Human thought, human pride, human ways and human works must be destroyed and the sinner must submit to the will and way of God (James 4:6; Matt. 8:1-3).

Consider the following points, and you will see how Naaman typifies sinners whom the Lord is pleased to save.

1. Naaman had many commendable human traits but *something was wrong,* seriously wrong, which made everything he was and had useless (v. 1). He was a great man among men, honourable and mighty in valour, but he was a leper! Disease and death flowed through his veins, incurable by human means.

There are fleshly differences among men, making some wiser, stronger, richer, or more honourable than others; but all men have one thing in common which makes all that they are and have useless. 'All have sinned, and come short of the glory of God' (Rom 3:23). Sin and death are within us by birth, nature and choice, and are incurable by human means (Eph. 2:11-12; Gal. 3:10; Rom. 5:12).

Our sinful nature makes even our righteousnesses filthy rags (Isa. 64:6).

2. Naaman sought help, but *he took the wrong things with him* (v. 5). Being conscious of his condition and hearing that there was a possibility of healing in the land of Israel, he went forth with a letter of recommendation from his employer and gold, silver and presents for his benefactor. He came to Israel to buy deliverance.

Before we judge Naaman too harshly, let us examine today's religious attempts to find favour with God. Is it not the way of natural man to work, merit, or try to earn salvation? (Matt. 7:21-22; Mark 10:17). Instead of coming to the Lord Jesus as guilty sinners with nothing in our hands, we come bearing our morality, our works, our baptism and our church membership. Men say, 'I'm no worse than others.' Naaman was no more a leper than other lepers, but he was a leper, and we are sinners! God's way of salvation is Christ alone. All that God requires and all that the sinner needs are fulfilled in Christ (Col. 2:9-10; 1 Cor. 1:30; Gal. 4:4-5).

3. Naaman *went to the wrong place* (vv. 6-7). Instead of going to the prophet of God, as he was told by the little maid (v. 3), he went to the king. This prophet of God represents Christ, who is our Prophet, Priest and King (Deut. 18:17-19; Heb. 1:1-2).

Salvation is of the Lord in its origination, execution, application, sustaining power and ultimate perfection. How foolish it is to turn to the virgin Mary, to the priest, to the preacher, to the law, or to the church, when Christ, our Lord, says, 'If any man thirst, let him come to me'! (John 7:37-39; 14:6). Why do men look to those who cannot save, instead of looking to the only true God? (Isa. 45:20-22).

4. When Naaman finally came to the prophet of God, *he came with the wrong attitude* (vv. 8-9). See him stand proudly outside the humble dwelling of Elisha. He wanted to be treated as a great man who happened to have leprosy, when in reality he was only a leper who happened to be a great man. Elisha knew his pride and arrogance and would not come out to meet him, but instructed him to strip off his earthly garb of glory and wash in the muddy Jordan seven times. How degrading this appeared to Naaman!

Sinners today want special recognition, special attention and the praise and honour of men, even in their religious professions (John

5:42-44). Pride of face, pride of race, pride of place and even pride of grace prevail. We, like Naaman, want to be treated as great ones who happen to be sinners, instead of what we are — sinners who, for a while, have certain status among worms. There is none good nor righteous (Rom. 3:10-11).

5. Naaman *had wrong thoughts about mercy* (vv. 11-12). He said, **'I thought, He will surely come out to me and stand, and call on ... his God.'** Naaman's way (which would preserve his own pride and position) and God's way (which would humble the proud leper and give God all the glory) were opposites.

Salvation by free grace, through the righteousness and cross of the Lord Jesus, is offensive to natural man (1 Cor. 1:18-24). Our thoughts are not God's thoughts and our ways are not God's ways (Isa. 55:6-9). Total depravity offends man's dignity, divine revelation offends man's wisdom and the blood of the cross offends man's pride. God will humble us before himself, or he will destroy us.

6. Naaman finally did something right — *he went down* (vv. 13-14). He came down off his high horse and bowed to the way of God.

When sinners are ready and made willing (Ps. 110:3) to quit lying, trying and buying and bow to the Lord Jesus Christ and receive salvation as the free gift of God, they will be saved (Matt. 5:3-6; 9:10-13).

Questions

1. Naaman wanted to be healed. Today many people would like their sin forgiven. Is wanting forgiveness enough?
2. List some examples of 'wrong' attempts to get forgiveness.
3. How can true forgiveness and cleansing from God be obtained?

39. 'Open his eyes that he may see'

2 Kings 6:8-23

The King of Syria made war against Israel. Calling together a council of his servants, he made plans to camp in a certain place and ambush the King of Israel. Elisha sent word to the king to take another route. Each time that the Syrians secretly planned to attack them, Elisha warned Israel and they escaped. Finally, the King of Syria was convinced that he had a traitor among his servants, who was leaking information to Israel. One of his servants said, 'There is no traitor; but Elisha, the prophet in Israel, tells the King of Israel everything, even what you say in your bedroom.' The King of Syria was told that Elisha was in Dothan; so he sent horses, chariots and a large army to surround the city and capture Elisha. Elisha's servant got up early and went out of the house. Seeing the great army of the enemy surrounding them, he cried unto Elisha, **'Alas, my master, [what] shall we do?'** Elisha calmly replied, **'Fear not: they that be with us are more than they that be with them.'** This is what King Hezekiah told the people of Judah when the King of Assyria came against them: 'With him is an arm of flesh; but with us is the Lord our God to help us, and to fight our battles' (2 Chron. 32:7-8).

When we truly know the Scriptures and the power of God, there is no reason to fear what men can do (Matt. 22:29; Ps. 56:3-4). We do not underestimate the power of Satan, sin and the world, but our God is greater than all and he will deliver us. However, the greatness, grace and power of God to redeem and deliver sinners, in and through the Lord Jesus Christ, from the overwhelming curse of the law, from the power of sin and Satan and from death, judgement and hell, is only seen with the eyes of faith (Matt. 13:15-16). Elisha prayed that God would open the young man's eyes that he might see. May God open our eyes that we may see.

1. *The natural eye is blind to spiritual truth* as the natural ear does not hear and the natural heart does not understand (1 Cor. 2:9-14; Isa. 64:4). Men read the Word of God with a veil over their eyes and minds. Sinners pass, blindfolded by sin, through all the testimonies of redeeming love and grace and see them not, nor hear them.

> God is everywhere, but the blind see him not.
> His great law touches the thoughts and intents of the heart, but men do not see.
> Men themselves are guilty, fallen and far from God, but they do not see their wounds, bruises and putrefying sores.
> Death, judgement and hell move to meet men at their coming, but they see not. They dance blindly on the edge of hell.
> The Lord Jesus came into the world to save sinners, but they saw no beauty about him and knew him not.
> Natural blindness keeps a man content in filth, false refuges and spiritual poverty.
> Natural blindness makes men proud, for they do not see their ignorance nor his glory.

Only God can open a sinner's eyes, for the hearing ear and the seeing eye are of the Lord (Prov. 20:12). We may put truth before men, but only God can make them to see (Isa. 42:6-8; 2 Cor. 4:6; Ps. 146:8). Once Satan promised to open a man's eyes, but the man saw shame, not glory (Gen. 3:5-7).

2. *The Lord does open men's eyes* and by his grace give them spiritual sight and understanding. **'And the Lord opened the eyes of the young man; and he saw'** (v. 17).

The eye of faith *sees what others do not see!* Noah saw the flood coming (Heb. 11:7). The disciples saw the deity of Jesus Christ (Matt. 16:13-17). Isaiah complained about the blindness of men, but the Ethiopian saw the glory of Christ when Philip preached Christ from Isaiah's account of his sufferings (Isa. 53:1-6).

The eye of faith *produces a calm spirit of assurance.* The servant in our story was afraid and cried, 'Alas, master! What shall we do?'

But Elisha was not afraid, for he saw the army of the Lord and was confident of deliverance. Job was confident of God's care even in the deepest trial (Job 1:20-22).

The eye of faith *does not grow dim with the passing of years* but sees better. The young man saw the enemy but no Redeemer; he saw danger and no deliverance. The old prophet had seen the glory and grace of God often and, like Abraham, he knew, 'The Lord will provide.' With age and maturity come better sight and understanding (2 Peter 3:18).

The eye of faith *desires to see more* (John 5:20).

> More of the wonders of his Word (Ps. 119:18).
> More of Christ, the Lord (Phil. 3:8-10).
> More of his righteousness revealed in the gospel (Rom. 1:16-17).
> More of his redemptive glory (Exod. 33:18-19).
> And the blessed hope of saving faith is to see him and to awake with his likeness (1 John 3:2-3; Ps. 17:15; 27:4).

One important thing to remember is that, like Hagar's well in the desert (Gen. 21:19), deliverance is there in Christ all the time; we only need spiritual eyes to see.

Questions

1. When sin makes war against the people of God, where can deliverance be found?
2. What does 'open a sinner's eyes' mean? Who opens them?
3. What is faith?

40. Four lepers

2 Kings 6:24 - 7:8

The city of Samaria had been surrounded by the Syrian army for a long time, and there was a great famine in the city so that an ass's head sold for eighty pieces of silver (2 Kings 6:24-25). Food was so scarce that people were eating human flesh (vv. 26-29). The King of Israel was so upset that he threatened to kill Elisha, God's prophet (v. 31). He came, leaning on the hand of one of his lords, to see Elisha, and Elisha told the king that food would be so plentiful in Samaria by tomorrow that flour and barley would be sold very cheaply (2 Kings 7:1). The lord, upon whose hand the king leaned, told Elisha that this was impossible and that he did not believe it, to which Elisha replied, 'Oh yes, you will see it all; but you will not eat of it' (2 Kings 7:2,16-20).

On the day that the king came to Elisha, there were four men with leprosy sitting at the gate of the city, and they said to one another, 'Why do we sit here and starve to death? If we sit here, we shall die; if we go into the city, we shall die, for there is no food there. The thing for us to do is to go to our enemies, the Syrians, and seek mercy. If they show mercy and spare us, we shall live; but if they kill us, we shall but die' (vv. 3-4). So they arose that evening and entered the camp of the Syrians but, to their surprise, they found no one there. They found abundant food, drink, clothes, silver and gold, but all the Syrians had fled (vv. 5-8). That evening the Lord had made all the Syrians to hear the noise of chariots, horses and a mighty army advancing, and the Syrians, thinking that the King of Israel had persuaded the Egyptians and Hittites to come against them, had fled, leaving all of their supplies behind.

Why is this story in the Word of God, and how does it teach us redemption in Jesus Christ?

1. These diseased, dying, starving lepers represent *the whole human race under the judgement and curse of sin.* Spiritually we are wretched, miserable, poor, blind and naked (Rev. 3:17). We are without Christ, without hope and without God in this world (Eph. 2:11-12).

There is no way adequately to describe the total ruin, utter poverty and spiritual helplessness and hopelessness of Adam's sons (Rom. 3:10-19; 5:12). These starving, helpless lepers do give us a dim picture of our spiritual condition. Only the Spirit of God can reveal to sinners what happened in the Garden of Eden and the terrible consequences upon us all and cause us to cry with Isaiah, 'I am undone; I am cut off' (Isa. 1:4-6; 6:5; 64:6).

2. The lepers, knowing their helpless state, considered three alternatives: 'If we *stay here*, we shall die; if we *go into the city*, we shall die, for they have no food; or the Syrians are our enemies, but they have plenty of food. We can *go to them and seek mercy and help.* If they choose to show mercy to us, we shall live; but if not, we have lost nothing, for we shall die anyway. Wisely they chose to cast themselves on the mercy of the Syrians, and they were delivered by the providence of God.

Considering our hopeless, sinful state (Jer. 13:23; Gal. 3:10), what is there for us to do?

If we stay where we are, we shall perish under the wrath of God (Heb. 9:27). Salvation is impossible with men. Our condition only worsens as we become hardened in sin.

If we go into the city, we shall die there. What can the city represent but organized religion — man's organized efforts to help himself? (Rom. 10:1-4). The city had people, activity, buildings and organizations, but they had no food, for themselves or for anyone else (Amos 8:11-12). When the Master asked the disciples, 'Will you also go away?' they replied, 'Lord, to whom shall we go?' Men have nothing to offer; the law has nothing to offer; religion has nothing to offer except a refuge of lies (Isa. 28:14-15).

We can cast ourselves on the mercy of God. Even though we have sinned against God and our sins have brought his wrath and judgement, God is merciful (Isa. 59:2; Ps. 130:3-4). While it is true that all are children of wrath, even as others, and God is angry with the wicked, the Lord delights to show mercy (Micah 7:18-19; Rom. 5:6-10; Eph. 2:2-7).

When the lepers decided to turn to the only possible source of relief, they reasoned, 'It may be that they will save us alive.' Men of wisdom have used this reasoning before in reference to God's mercy — Jonathan (1 Sam. 14:6), David (2 Sam. 16:11-12), the King of Nineveh (Jonah 3:8-9). God is certainly not obligated to save anyone, but those who know their sin in the light of his holiness and are persuaded to look to him and cast themselves on his mercy in Christ Jesus always find plenteous redemption.

There are several reasons to have a good hope for mercy when one comes to the Lord God in repentance and faith.

1. It is the gracious nature of God to show mercy (Exod. 34:6-7; Micah 7:18-19).
2. The Lord Jesus came into the world to save sinners (Gal. 4:4-5; Luke 19:10; 1 Tim. 1:15).
3. By his righteousness and sacrifice, Christ enables God to be both a just God and a Saviour (Rom. 3:25-26).
4. It is the chief glory of God to save (Exod. 33:18-19).
5. It is the command of God for us to come to him, and with the command comes the warrant to believe (Isa. 45:21-22; 1 John 3:23).

How long will a beggar sit by the road and wait for a hand-out? How long will a fisherman cast his hook into the water? How long will a father seek a lost son? And how long should sinners seek mercy when the outlook is so bright? (Jer. 29:13-14).

Questions
1. Why is the image of a starving leper a good analogy of a sinner outside Christ?
2. Do you agree that God is not obligated to save anyone? What does this mean?
3. What is the basis of 'a good hope for mercy'?

41. Nehushtan — 'a piece of brass'

2 Kings 18:1-8

King Hezekiah was twenty-five years old when he began to reign over Judah. He reigned twenty-nine years in Jerusalem. Compared to that of his father, Ahaz, and others, his was a good reign.

> **'He did that which was right in the sight of the Lord, according to all that David, his father** [i.e. ancestor] **did'** (v. 3).
> **'He trusted in the Lord God of Israel.'** None of the Kings of Judah, before or after him, reigned so well (v. 5).
> **'He clave to the Lord, and ... kept his commandments... And the Lord was with him'** and prospered him (vv. 6-7).

In this account of the good reign of Hezekiah, one verse stands out above all the rest and demands our special attention. Verse 4 declares that **'[Hezekiah] removed the high places, and brake the images, and cut down the groves, and brake in pieces the brazen serpent that Moses had made.'** The Jews say that he ground the brazen serpent to powder and scattered it to every wind, that there might be no remains of it!

In those days, 'The children of Israel did evil in the sight of the Lord,' married heathens and worshipped their gods, serving Baalim and the groves (cf. Judges 3:7). The high places were temples and shrines built on mountains for idol worship. The images, or statues, were, like the golden calf, idol gods. The groves were wooded areas dedicated to idolatry, where altars were erected to gods. Jupiter was worshipped in a grove of oaks and Apollo in a grove of laurels.

Hezekiah destroyed all of these high places, groves and statues —
something his father and other Kings of Judah had not dared to do.
But he also utterly destroyed the brazen serpent which Moses had
made in the wilderness (Num. 21:5-8). The Israelites had brought
this serpent into the land of Canaan and, as it was made by Moses,
they imagined it might be of some service to them towards God.
Some say they did not worship it but only burned incense to it and
used it in religious activities. Hezekiah knew they were ensnared by
this memorial and even drawn into idolatry by it; so he destroyed the
serpent, calling it **'Nehushtan'** — 'a worthless piece of brass'.

I can understand a person's interest in that brazen serpent. It
would be extremely interesting to see the serpent which Moses
made and lifted up. Our God used that serpent as a type of the
crucified Redeemer (the Lord Jesus himself referred to it) and on
that occasion healed all who looked to it. It would be interesting to
see the rod of Moses, the tables of the law, the tabernacle, the ark of
the covenant and the smitten rock. But interesting is all it would be
— certainly not inspirational, nor edifying, nor of any spiritual
value, nor of any consequence where our relationship with God is
concerned. In the worship of God, Christ is all (John 14:6; 1 Cor.
1:30; Col. 1:12-20; 2:9-10). Believers believe, love and worship
God in Spirit, not in form, rituals, nor with visual aids. They rejoice
only in Christ Jesus and have no confidence in the flesh (Phil. 3:3).
True believers have no superstitions regarding days, hallowed
places, religious relics, symbols and signs, nor ancestors (Phil 3:4-
10). Christ is our sabbath, our sin offering, our High Priest, our altar,
our mediator, our Prophet, Priest and King. By his blood we
ourselves are made kings and priests to our God. We bow before no
man, make pilgrimages to no place on earth (our God is
everywhere), carry no religious symbols and place no merit
whatsoever in religious holidays such as Christmas and Easter. The
Lord has given his church two ordinances to observe until he
returns: baptism and the Lord's Table. In baptism believers confess
faith in Christ alone and identify publicly with him in his death,
burial and resurrection. In observing the Lord's Table with the
simple elements of bread and wine, we show forth his death until he
comes.

I am confident that the religious, supersitious Israelites were
shocked when King Hezekiah destroyed the brazen serpent which
Moses had made, called it a 'piece of brass' and declared it to be of

no value in the worship of God. But if we could find the actual cross on which Christ died, it would serve no purpose and must be called a 'piece of wood'. The grave in which Christ lay is but 'a hole in the ground', and the winding sheet in which he was wrapped is but a 'piece of cloth'. Idolatry is such a subtle thing of Satan and must be avoided at all costs. God is a jealous God and will not share his glory, or the worship and affection of his people. We trust, rest in and believe on the Lord Jesus Christ and abhor any effort to rob him of his pre-eminence. The lands around Jerusalem may be called the 'Bible lands' or whatever, but certainly not the 'Holy Land'. Let us be done with crosses, religious pictures of our Lord, shrines and uniforms of religion, and let us worship God in spirit, rejoice in Christ Jesus and put no confidence in the flesh. Christ, by his perfect obedience, has imputed unto us a perfect righteousness, and by his death we have the atonement. We are accepted in the Beloved. Nothing needs to be added to his person and work to bring us to God!

Questions
1. Why do rituals and religious symbols contradict true, living faith?
2. An idol need not be a carved piece of wood or a sculptured stone. What other examples of idolatry can you think of?
3. What are the practical implications of looking to Christ alone for salvation?

42. Bringing back the ark

1 Chronicles 13:1-14; 15:11-29

The ark of the covenant was an oblong chest of acacia wood, forty-five inches long, twenty-seven inches wide and twenty-seven inches deep. It contained the tables of the law, the pot of manna and Aaron's rod (Heb. 9:4). It was kept in the Holy of Holies, denoting the presence of God on the mercy seat, which was on the lid of the ark. During the days of Samuel, the superstitious Israelites took the ark from Shiloh into battle and lost it to the Philistines (1 Sam. 4:3-4,10-11). It was finally brought to Kirjath-Jearim, a city in the tribe of Judah, where it remained for fifty years.

13:1-3. David wanted the ark back in Jerusalem. He felt that the ark was an assurance of the presence of the Lord among his people, and where the ark was, there was the glory of God. So he consulted with the leaders and the people. Strange that David did not seek the mind of the Lord in this matter!

13:4-6. This seemed like a good idea to all the people, so David gathered together 30,000 chosen men, with instruments, singers and all of Israel, and they journeyed to Baalah, or Kirjath-Jearim, to bring up the ark.

13:7-8. This is an astonishing event. David was well versed in the law of God, as were the priests who were with him. They all knew that the ark was only to be carried by staves on the shoulders of the Levites. But David prepared a new cart with oxen, driven by Uzza and Ahio, to carry the ark of the covenant. After putting the ark on the cart, they began their journey to Jerusalem, rejoicing, singing, playing upon the instruments, confident that God was pleased with them.

13:9-10. When the procession came to the threshingfloor of Chidon, the oxen who were pulling the cart stumbled, and Uzza put out his hand to steady the ark, and God smote him dead because he put his hand on the ark.

13:11-14. The people were all stunned, and David was displeased because the Lord had smitten Uzza, but all of them (including David) realized, at last, that God was angry and displeased with the whole affair. So David put the ark in the house of Obed-edom, where it remained for three months.

What was wrong with this whole affair? Why was the Lord displeased with David and Israel? It would seem that David was doing the right thing in returning the ark of the covenant to Jerusalem and should be commended. David gives us the answer, three months later, when he determined again to bring up the ark (1 Chron. 15:12-13). Instead of going to the captains and the congregation (as he did the first time), this time David consulted with the priests of God. He said to them, 'You and your brethren sanctify yourselves that you may carry the ark into the place I have prepared for it. Because I ignored God's priests and put the ark on a cart, the Lord was angry with us. **We sought him not after the due order.**' In ignoring God's priests, it was as if David ignored the mediator. The high priest (who offered the atonement) and the other priests (who offered the sacrifices and ministered about the tabernacle) are types and pictures of our Lord Jesus Christ.

1. The priests were taken from among men and ordained for men in things pertaining to God (Heb. 5:1). So Christ was of the seed of David, according to the flesh, to be our mediator.

2. The priests were chosen of God, and no man took this honour unto himself (Heb. 5:4). So Christ glorified not himself to be our priest; the Father ordained him.

3. The priests offered sacrifices and the high priest offered the atonement once a year (Heb. 9:6-7). No man dared to

assume this office nor this duty; those who did perished. Even King Uzziah was struck with leprosy by the Lord when he attempted to offer a sacrifice without God's priest (2 Chron. 26:16-21).

Christ, our Lord, is our High Priest, our atonement and our mediator. No one comes to the Father but by him (John 14:6; 1 Tim. 2:5). Without question, this was David's error; and the Lord dealt severely with him and his friends. Knowing God's commandment in regard to the priests' carrying the ark (for that matter, moving it at all), David and the people sought to approach God, move and set up the ark and establish worship of the Lord without God's priest. This is a serious error. It does not matter how sincere we may be in desiring to worship God, know God, serve God, or approach God; he is only worshipped, known and approached in the Lord Jesus Christ! Cain built an altar and tried to worship God, but he ignored Christ and was rejected. King Saul ignored the prophet-priest and offered a sacrifice and was rejected of God.

15:14-15. Now David came to God the right way; the priests carried the ark.

15:25-26. God was pleased and helped the priests who bore the ark. They offered the blood sacrifice before the Lord. When David sought the first time to return the ark to Jerusalem, these two things were missing — the priests and the blood sacrifice (Heb. 10:19-22; 9:22).

15:27-29. We also have a humble King David, who took the place of a servant and danced before the ark borne on the shoulders of the priests (2 Sam. 6:14-16,20-22).

Questions
1. What is a mediator? How does Christ fulfil this office between God and men?
2. What are some modern equivalents of David transporting God's ark in a cart?
3. Is our sincerity before God an adequate mediator?

43. Uzziah's great transgression

2 Chronicles 26; Isaiah 6:1-5

Our study begins with Isaiah's vision in Isaiah 6:1-5.

v. 1. In the year that King Uzziah died, Isaiah saw the Lord (God the Son) sitting upon a throne, in the posture of a judge, to hear causes and execute judgement. His train, or the borders of his judicial robes, spread abroad and filled the temple.

v. 2. The seraphims (ministers and messengers of the Lord, bright and glorious, fervent in zeal for God's service and glory) covered their faces out of profound reverence, covered their feet, owning their own imperfections, and flew to execute God's commands.

v. 3. Here is the essence of the vision: **'One cried unto another and said, Holy, holy, holy, is the Lord of hosts.'** God is infinitely, eternally and immutably holy in all his ways. It is repeated for the greater assurance and establishment of the fact. If there is one attribute mentioned most frequently or one word used to emphasize the nature of our God, it is that 'God is *holy*', unapproachable by sinful creatures (1 Tim. 6:15-16).

v. 5. Isaiah's response to the vision was to declare, **'Woe is me!** I am cut off from God. I am an unclean branch of an unclean tree. I am a great sinner, especially by my lips, which reveal my heart. There is no hope for me nor those about me, before God's awful holy presence.'

Was there a connection between the death of King Uzziah and Isaiah's vision? Who was King Uzziah? What relationship did he have with Isaiah? How did he die? See 2 Chronicles 26.

v. 22. Isaiah was the prophet of God during the reign of Uzziah (Isa. 1:1). Isaiah wrote of the acts and rule of Uzziah from first to last.

vv. 1-4. Uzziah was a good king, who did that which was right in the sight of the Lord God. He sought the Lord, and God made him to prosper. God helped him in battle (vv. 7-8). He served the people, building towers in the desert to protect herds, digging many wells and planting vineyards (v. 10). He had a great army (vv. 12-13), was a brilliant leader (v. 15) and his name was known far and wide.

v. 16. But Uzziah made a serious and fatal mistake which led to his utter destruction and death. **'When he was strong,'** he was mighty, he was proud of his accomplishments, he was free from the fear of the enemy; and his heart was so overcome by his importance that he went into the temple, into the holy place, where the altar of incense stood, and into which none but the priest might enter, to offer incense himself upon the altar.

vv. 17-18. Azariah, the priest, and eighty priests of the Lord withstood King Uzziah, declaring unto him the seriousness of his act. Only the priests of God, the sons of Aaron, were consecrated by God to burn incense to the Lord. No man, not even a king, was permitted to offer sacrifices for sin (Heb. 5:1-5). They told him that such an act could not honour him before God. No matter how sincere nor how great a man may be, it is folly to violate the holiness of God.

vv. 19-21. Instead of listening to the priest and leaving the temple, Uzziah became angry and held to the censer to burn incense. God smote the proud king with leprosy, took away his office, and he died in disgrace as a common leper. When they buried him, they said, 'He is a leper.'

Isaiah evidently learned much from the death of King Uzziah. He said, 'In the year that King Uzziah died, I saw the Lord; I saw myself and I saw the condition of the people.'

God is holy. Our God is infinitely, indescribably holy in all his ways, acts and nature. He will in no wise clear the guilty nor receive any man apart from perfect holiness. He will not speak to, nor be spoken to by, any sinful creature. He is unapproachable except through the mediator.

Men are sinners. 'There is none that doeth good, no not one.' There is none righteous. Your sins have separated you and your God. 'Every imagination of the heart of man is evil continually.'

There is a way to God. Our God in mercy and grace has determined to redeem, sanctify and receive a people out of every tribe, kindred and tongue, but only in the way consistent with his holiness, righteousness and truth. He will be both just and justifier; he will be both merciful and righteous; he will be a just God and a Saviour (Isa. 45:20-25).

Christ is the way. Jesus Christ, the only begotten Son of God, came to earth made of woman, made under the law to redeem. He is our surety by divine decree; he is our righteousness by perfect obedience; he is our sacrifice, sin-offering and atonement by death; he is our risen justifier and our great High Priest, who intercedes at God's right hand. No man comes to God but by, in and through Christ Jesus (John 14:6).

The Old Testament priests, appointed and consecrated by God, were pictures and types of Christ, our great High Priest. They entered the Holy Place as Christ entered heaven; the incense they burned represented the prayers of Christ; the atonement they offered is the blood of Christ, and the fact that only the priest with a suitable sacrifice was accepted reveals that only Christ can effectually bring a sinner to God! When King Uzziah proceeded to usurp the authority of the priest and burn incense to God in the Holy Place, he was ignoring the Lord Jesus Christ and coming to God in his own person and works. For this great sin God destroyed him, as he will all who reject the Redeemer. Would you approach God for mercy, forgiveness and acceptance? Then receive, bow to and confess Christ Jesus. Do not come any other way (Heb. 10:11-22).

Questions

1. There are many men and women who apparently prosper in the church of Christ. Is such outward appearance dependable?
2. How do the four points made under paragraph 3 encapsulate the gospel?
3. What does it mean that Christ 'is our righteousness'?

44. Four things learned in trouble

Job 1:1-22

Job was greatly troubled, perhaps as few men in this world have been troubled. He had literally lost everything!

1. He was a man of *great wealth* (v. 3). Suddenly he was a man of complete poverty. Everything he owned was swept away (vv. 14-17).
2. He was a *family* man with ten children (v. 2). All of his children were killed in a storm (vv. 18-19). Even his wife turned against him (Job 2:9-10).
3. He was a man of *great influence*, with servants and many friends. Suddenly he was the laughing-stock of the city (Job 19:13-19).
4. He was a man of *strength and good health*. Now he was so frail and covered with boils that even his friends could scarcely recognize him (Job 2:7-8,12).

Job did not try to hide his sorrow; he wept before God. God's people are people with tender feelings, and when they are called upon to bear the rod, they feel it! God takes away our heart of stone; he does not turn the heart to stone. We sorrow, indeed, but not as those who have no hope.

Job's sorrow was sanctified by worship (vv. 20-22). Sorrow and trouble should always lead to worship and praise. In all of this trouble, trial and sorrow, Job did not speak in an unworthy manner against God. He did not dishonour the name of God, nor compare his lot with the lot of others. He fell down and worshipped God (Job

2:10; 13:15). If grief presses you to the ground, worship there. If trials lay you low, worship there (Ps. 62:8).

Times of trial should not only be times of worship, but also times for teaching and consideration. Listen to David talking to himself in the time of trouble (Ps. 42:5-11). Job, by his words, reveals to us that he was a man of faith, well taught in the things of God. Four things are seen.

1. He knew the brevity of life

'Naked I came into the world and naked I shall return.' This was Job's idea of life and a very true one. 'I came and I shall return' (Job. 14:1-5). Our life on earth is in the Scripture compared to a flower (Job 14:2), a vapour (James 4:14), a weaver's shuttle (Job 7:6) and a post (Job 9:25) — that is, an outpost on a mail delivery where the rider changes horses. Not only in time of sorrow, but at all times, we need to consider the brevity of life on earth and the length of life to come and find our joy and hope in our Redeemer (Job 19:23-27; Phil. 1:20-24).

2. He knew the frailty of earthly possessions

The word is 'naked'. When a baby is born into this world, what does he possess? He possesses nothing; he comes into the world naked! When a man dies, what does he possess? What does he take with him? He leaves the world naked! The Lord teaches Job (and those who will learn by his example) the frailty and vanity of all that we have in our hands and all that we call our own. Actually, we brought nothing into this world and we shall carry nothing out (1 Tim. 6:7). However, we can leave this world differently from the way we came. We were born sinners (Ps. 51:5; 58:3). By God's grace and mercy, through faith in Christ Jesus, we can leave justified, redeemed and free from sin (Acts 13:38-39; John 3:14-16). Without Christ we shall die as we were born — lost sinners!

3. He saw the hand of God in all things

'The Lord gave, and the Lord hath taken away.' Many people reading this portion of Scripture would say that Satan afflicted Job and took away all that he possessed, but Job (like every true believer) knew that the Lord is the first cause of all things. Satan and other second causes can only do what God is pleased to permit them to do (1 Sam. 2:6-8; Acts 4:27-28; Isa. 46:9-11).

'The Lord *gave.*' Job did not say, 'I earned these things; I deserve them, for they are the products of my hard work.' No! He said, 'All that I have is the gift of God.' 'A man can receive nothing, except it be given him from heaven' (John 3:27; 1 Cor. 4:7). All that I have physically, mentally, materially and spiritually is the gift of God. Even repentance towards God and faith in the Lord Jesus Christ are the gifts of God (Rom. 2:4; Acts 11:18; Eph. 2:8-9; Phil. 1:29).

'The Lord *hath taken away.*' Job saw the hand of God in all that was taken. He did not curse the Sabeans, or the wicked Chaldeans, and blame the wind. He knew that the Lord God controlled all these things and that the Lord God had willed it, or it would not have happened (Rom. 8:28). Aaron held his peace when his sons were killed, for he knew the Lord had done it (Lev. 10:1-3; cf. 1 Sam. 3:18; Ps. 39:9).

4. He declared that in all things, at all times, God is to be praised

'Blessed be the name of the Lord.' To be able to praise God equally in the valley of trial as on the mountain of joy ought to be the desire of every believer (1 Cor. 16:13-14). Paul sounds this note in 1 Thessalonians 5:18. He writes, 'In everything,' loss or gain, sickness or health, success or failure, summer or winter, life or death, 'give thanks: for this [whatever it be, if you are in Christ] is the will of God in Christ Jesus concerning you.'

Questions
1. Why is it important to recognize God's hand in all our circumstances, good and bad?
2. What would be the implication if God were not the first cause of all events?
3. What is the basis of Job's contention that in all things, and at all times, God is to be praised?

45. 'How can man be just with God?'

Job 9:2; 15:14-16; 25:4-6

This question is asked over and over by Job and his friends. **'How should man be just with God?'** (Job. 9:2). **'What is man, that he should be clean? And he which is born of a woman, that he should be righteous?'** (Job 15:14). **'How then can man be justified with God?'** (Job 25:4).

This question of questions arises from an understanding of three things: the holiness of God, the sinfulness of men and what it means to be justified.

1. God's chief attribute is holiness

If there is one word used to describe our God, it is 'holy' (Isa. 6:1-5). 'Holy and reverend is his name.' 'The Lord is in his temple' (Ps. 111:9; Hab. 2:20; Ps. 99:3; Zeph. 1:7). Everything about God and having to do with our God is said to be holy: his holy angels; his Holy Spirit; his presence was manifested in the Holy of Holies; on the mitre of the high priest were the words 'Holiness to the Lord,' and without holiness no man shall see the Lord (Heb. 12:14). When God manifests his grace, mercy and love, it must be in keeping with his holiness. God is holy!

How holy is God? So holy that a fallen Adam must be separated from his presence; so holy that Moses could not look upon him and live; so holy that Uzza was smitten dead for touching the ark; so holy that the seraphims covered their faces before him; so holy that Isaiah, upon discovering God's holiness, cried, 'I am cut off'; so holy that he deserted his beloved Son, when he was bearing our sins on the cross.

2. *The word that most accurately describes man is 'sinner'*

Man was not created a sinner. He was created holy and upright, but he became a sinner through the Fall (Rom. 5:12,19). He is 'born in sin' (Ps. 51:5; 58:3) and incapable of any good in the flesh (Jer. 13:23; Rom. 8:8).

How sinful is man? 'Every imagination of the thoughts of his heart [is] only evil continually' (Gen. 6:5). 'They are all together become filthy' (Ps. 14:1-3). 'There is none righteous ... none that doeth good' (Rom. 3:10-19). The Scriptures declare that men are dead, having no hope and without God in this world (Eph. 2:1,12). Men may seek to justify themselves (Luke 16:15) and compare themselves with themselves (2 Cor. 10:12), but in God's sight, 'Every mouth [must] be stopped, and all the world ... become guilty... Therefore, by the deeds of the law there shall no flesh be justified' (Rom. 3:19-20).

3. *What does it mean to be justified before God?*

To be justified is to be without sin, guilt or blame, 'just as if I had never sinned,' 'holy and unblameable and unreproveable in his sight' (Col. 1:22).

To be justified is to have perfect peace with God (Rom. 5:1).

To be justified is to be free from the curse of the law and free from all charges (Rom. 8:33).

To be justified is to have eternal life and glory (Rom. 8:30).

To be justified is to be totally reconciled to God (Rom. 5:10).

Therefore, in view of the holiness of God, the sinfulness and inability of men and what it means to be justified, clean and righteous before God, the question is asked again and again, 'How can man be justified in God's sight?' How can God be just and justify sinners? A man cannot be justified by words (Job 9:20). He cannot be justified by law (Gal. 3:10-11). He cannot be justified by works (Titus 3:5). Then how can man be just with God?

4. The answer is found in Romans 3:21-26

v. 21. **'The righteousness of God'** is not God's own personal holiness, but that righteousness he has, by his grace, provided for, and imputed to guilty sinners through his Son (Rom. 10:1-4). The righteousness of God signifies both the precept of the law and the penalty of the law, Christ having honoured every precept in his perfect life and satisfied every debt in his death. **'Without the law'** simply means without the sinner's obeying the law, for this Christ certainly did for us. It **'is manifested'** in the gospel (Rom. 1:16-17). Why is the gospel the power of God unto salvation? Because in, through and by Christ, this righteousness of God is revealed. All we need is accomplished and set forth in the gospel.

vv. 22-23. This righteousness of God is accomplished by the faithfulness of Christ and imputed to those who believe. As the representative man (Rom. 5:19; 1 Cor. 15:21-22,47), God was made of woman, made under the law and perfectly obeyed it in order that all whom he represented might have a perfect holiness and standing before God (Gal. 4:4-5; Rom. 4:17-25). There is no difference between Jew, Gentile, male or female; all have sinned.

vv. 24-25. Those who believe are made righteous in Christ and are freely and fully justified by his obedience and death, even believers of Old Testament times; for Christ is also the propitiation for their sins.

v. 26. Christ came to earth in the flesh as the surety of God's eternal covenant, obeyed the law and died for all our sins in order that the holy God might be just and justifier of all who believe. He is 'a just God and a Saviour' (Isa. 45:21-22). This, dear friends, is the very heart of the gospel of God's glory, for it manifests and magnifies every attribute of our holy God. In Christ, our substitute, 'Mercy and truth are met together; righteousness and peace have kissed each other' (Ps. 85:10).

Questions
1. What makes the justification of man before God no mean feat?
2. How can the opposite extremes of God's holiness and man's wickedness be reconciled?
3. Why is Christ called our substitute?

46. Three vital questions

Job 14:1-14

In this study we shall consider chiefly three questions asked by Job which are answered only in our Lord Jesus Christ. The questions are: **'Who can bring a clean thing out of an unclean?'** (v. 4). **'Yea, man giveth up the ghost, and where is he?'** (v. 10). **'If a man die, shall he live again?'** (v. 14).

1. 'Who can bring a clean thing out of an unclean?'

v. 1. **'Man that is born of a woman.'** This is the cause of all our misery. We are the product, the offspring of natural, sinful parents. The first man (and the only man not born of woman) was created in the image of God. That man fell and became a sinful creature (Rom. 5:12,19; 1 Cor. 15:21-22). All who are born of woman are born in sin, frail, weak and of an evil nature (Ps. 51:5; 58:3). Sinful parents produce sinful offspring.

    'Is of few days, and full of trouble.' Before the flood some men lived as men as long as 900 years, but now and since the days of Moses, the years of men are but threescore and ten (Ps. 90:10). Those who live the longest live only a few days compared with eternity. Man is born to trouble because he is born in sin; sin and trouble go together! Sin, uncleanness, death and trouble live in and with this man born of woman.

v. 2. **'He cometh forth like a flower, and is cut down.'** As the flower comes from the earth, so does man; as the flower flourishes for a while and looks beautiful, so does man; as the flower soon

withers and dies, so does man. **'He fleeth also as a shadow, and
continueth not.'** A shadow is an empty thing, dark and without
substance, uncertain and quickly passing away, and so it fitly
resembles the life of a man (James 4:14).

v. 3.   Job has described all men in the preceding verses; but here he
refers mainly to himself and asks, 'Lord, do you open your eyes
upon such an unclean, worthless, temporary piece of clay?' Do you
take thought or care about him? Do you observe all his ways when
it is beneath you to contend with him? David considered this
question (Ps. 8:3-4). 'Lord', asks Job, 'do you bring me into
judgement with you?' No man can contend with God upon the basis
of strict justice (Ps. 143:2). Men do not even deserve to be
considered by God in the matter of righteousness and judgement.

v. 4.   **'Who can bring a clean thing out of an unclean? Not one.'**
We are born unclean, live unclean and die unclean in God's sight.
How can he be clean that is born of a woman? (Job 15:14-16; 25:4-
6). The answer is found in the Lord Jesus Christ, our Redeemer and
Saviour.

> Our Lord Jesus is the surety of a better covenant (Heb.
> 7:22; 13:20-21).
> Our Lord Jesus was born of a woman as our representative
> (Gal. 4:4-5). He had no human father, so was without the sin
> of Adam (1 Cor. 15:47-48).
> Our Lord Jesus, by his perfect obedience in the flesh,
> imputed to us a perfect holiness, sanctification and righteous-
> ness (Rom. 5:19; 3:19-24).
> Our Lord Jesus died for all our sins, cleansing us, perfect-
> ing us and presenting us holy in God's sight (1 John 1:7; Heb.
> 10:14; Col. 1:21-23).

2. 'Man giveth up the ghost, and where is he?'

vv. 7-9.   If a tree is cut down, it falls to earth, the root withers and the
branches and stock die in the ground. But if it rains on the remains of
that tree and the sun shines upon it, it will bud and grow again.

v. 10.   **'But a man dieth, and wasteth away.'** We die, are buried in the ground and go back to the dust from whence we came. There will be no revival of life because 'man giveth up the spirit'. Life is utterly gone! Where is he? The answer is found in our Lord Jesus Christ.

Our Lord said to the unbelieving thief, 'Today shalt thou be *with me* in paradise.' The believer who dies goes to be with the Lord Jesus. His body returns to the dust but his soul to God who gave it (Phil. 1:20-23; 2 Cor. 5:8).

Paul writes of our dwelling after death. He does not describe it but says, 'When we put off this tent we have a building of God' (2 Cor. 5:1-3). Moses and Elijah appeared in a certain form and talked with Christ (Luke 9:30-31).

3. *'If a man die, shall he live again?'*

v. 12. **'So man lieth down'** in the grave when he dies, **'and riseth not'**; or he will never come forth from that grave into the world, to the place where he was and as he was. The sense is that a man who dies will never live again as to this natural life, but he will indeed live again.

v. 14. **'If a man die, shall he live again?'** Oh, yes! Those who are in Christ have the promise of the glorious resurrection unto eternal life. 'Because I live, ye shall live,' says our Lord.

Our Lord Jesus died and rose again; so shall we (1 Cor. 15:12-22).

We shall have a glorified body like his (1 John 3:1-3; 1 Cor. 15:42-49).

How are the dead raised? (1 Cor. 15:35-38; Luke 24:36-43). Christ is the resurrection and the life. If we believe in him, we shall never die. We died when he died, arose in him and are seated with him in the heavenly places. We shall sleep but never die!

Questions
1. Why is God's justice a fearful prospect for man?
2. Is there life after death? Where will you spend it?
3. Jesus said, 'Because I live, ye shall live.' What does this mean?

47. 'I know that my Redeemer liveth'

Job 19:21-27

Suppose I took you to a fine home in the suburbs, beautifully landscaped; the mother is in the kitchen preparing the evening meal, there are healthy children playing in the garden, and the father returns home with the news that he has been promoted and given a rise. As they all gather about the table that evening to give thanks and the father says, 'The hand of God has touched me,' you would probably agree with him. But here in Job is a true believer, whom God called 'my servant, one that feareth God and shuns evil,' who was once wealthy but is now poor, once healthy but now sick, once powerful and influential but now alone and deserted (Job 19:9-20), and he says, **'The hand of God hath touched me.'** He did not say, 'Satan hath touched me,' but he declared, 'God hath touched me.'

This is a mystery that natural men do not understand, only those who have been touched first in regeneration by God (1 Cor. 2:7-14). In the natural world the way up is up, but in the spiritual world the way up is down. 'He that humbleth himself shall be exalted' (Luke 14:11). In the natural world, to live is to live, but in the spiritual world the way to live is to die (Matt. 10:39). In the natural world men find satisfaction in their own strength, but Paul declared, 'When I am *weak*, then I am strong' (2 Cor. 12:10). The greatest thing God can do for a person (whatever the cost) is to show him in heart and soul the vanity of all things in this world (Eccles. 1:2,14) and to turn his interest, affection, love and concern from the world to Christ (Matt. 5:3-12). To be full is to be emptied of self, to be wise is to become a fool for Christ's sake, to be clothed is to be stripped, to receive is to give, to reign is to serve and to be rich is to become poor.

This was Job's experience. He knew what it was to possess all that the world can afford; then he felt the full impact of watching it all fade away and being reduced to ashes! With everything gone, in the dust, at the bottom, with no place to hide and no arm to lean upon, he rejoices in the sinner's only hope — his Redeemer! (Ps. 73:25). Several things stand out in Job's testimony concerning Christ, our Redeemer.

1. Job had absolute certainty in an uncertain world

He could say, 'I *know* that my Redeemer liveth.' Like Abraham, Job believed God's Word. 'All flesh is grass, and all the goodliness thereof is as the flower of the field ... but the word of our God shall stand for ever' (Isa. 40:6-8). There is nothing certain in this world but its destruction, but we know that God is, that God is in Christ, and that God is in Christ reconciling us to himself (Heb. 11:6; 2 Cor. 5:19; 1 John 5:20).

2. Job had a true friend among false friends

'I know that my Redeemer liveth.' This is the word that stands out from all the rest. There is no name of the Messiah which is more significant, more comprehensive, nor more endearing than Redeemer.

The word signifies 'a near kinsman who has the right to redeem'. This is what the book of Ruth is all about — the kinsman redeemer! He has the right to redeem, being a near kinsman; he has the will to redeem because he loves; he has the price to redeem.

This is what Job is saying about our Lord Jesus Christ:

1. He has the right to redeem in that he took our flesh and was numbered with transgressors.
2. He has the will to redeem, for he loves us with an everlasting love.
3. He paid the full price with his own blood (1 Peter 1:18-19).

3. Job had the promise of life eternal even in a land of death

'I know that my Redeemer *liveth*.'

Our Redeemer was then living, for he is the same yester-
day, today and for ever. He 'was in the beginning with God'
(John 1:1).

Our Redeemer liveth because he is the life (John 1:4;
14:6).

Our Redeemer died and rose again and lives for ever (Rev.
1:17-18). Because he lives we shall live also, for his is 'the
resurrection and the life'.

*4. Job had the promise of victory over the grave and a real
inheritance on the new earth*

v. 25. He will stand on the earth. He once walked this earth as our
representative and sin-offering. He will come again and stand upon
the new earth, and we shall stand with him (John 14:1-3).

v. 26. 'Though I shall die,' Job declared, 'and this body shall go
back to dust, yet I shall rise from the grave and I shall see him in his
glory as one of his redeemed ones' (1 John 3:1-3).

v. 27. Job expected to be raised from the grave himself and with a
glorified body to live for ever with his Redeemer (1 Cor. 15:50-57).

Questions

1. Why are there so many contradictions between the values of a
natural man and a spiritual man?
2. What is the source of a believer's assurance?
3. How valuable is the promise of eternal life?

48. 'Now mine eye seeth thee'

Job 42:1-6

Let us begin by establishing some things that we know: Job was a man of integrity and uprightness, and one who feared the Lord (Job 1:8). Job was a man of great patience, reverence and dedication (Job 1:20-22). Job was a man of faith and perseverance (Job 13:15-16). Job was a man of sound theology (Job 19:23-27).

God, in his divine wisdom and good providence, had permitted all these trials to come upon Job — the loss of property and wealth, the loss of children and health and the loss of influence and standing. Job's three friends had come from afar to enquire of him concerning the evil he had done to deserve such tribulation (Job 2:11-13; 4:7; 8:2-6). Job defended himself rather strongly to his friends. They insisted that these tragedies would not have occurred if he were not guilty of some great sin. Job strongly denied their charges and claimed to be righteous (Job. 31:6; 32:1-2). Then came Elihu and rebuked both Job and his three friends: Job, because he justified himself rather than God, and his friends because they condemned Job without cause (Job 32:1-3).

After all these things, God spoke to Job (Job 38-41). The Lord had been silent during the trials, during the days of discussion and argument between Job and his friends and even as Elihu corrected them all. But now the Lord speaks to Job and declares, 'Who is this that darkeneth counsel by words without knowledge?' (Job 38:3; 42:3). 'Gird up your loins like a real man, for I have some things to show you and to enquire of you' (Job 38:3). If we read these chapters, we shall see God revealing himself to Job in his absolute sovereignty, infinite wisdom, infinite holiness, unchanging purpose and his total rule and reign over everything, from the greatest planet to the invisible atom, over all creatures and all their actions, and we shall see that he gives no account to anyone.

Then comes forth this tremendous confession from the lips of Job (Job 42:1-6).

'I know that thou canst do everything.' I am sure that Job had always believed in the power of God to do all things, but now it was not the sovereignty of God that Job saw, but the God who is sovereign. The power of God was now an experience, not a doctrine.

'No thought can be withholden from thee.' When will men cease to call him Lord with their lips while their hearts are far from him? Only when they see the Lord and learn that he looks on and knows the hearts and thoughts of all. No doubt Job's doctrinal position admitted the omniscience of God before this revelation, but now he has experienced it. It is doubtful if a person really believes anything until he experiences it. God revealed himself to Job; Job truly saw the Lord and was now able to understand that 'God is not worshipped with hands,' holy days, outward form and righteousness, but from the heart in spirit and truth, for the living God knows the thoughts and motives of men. 'My son, give me thine heart' (Prov. 23:26; Rom. 10:9-10).

'Who is he that hideth counsel without knowledge?' Who is it who darkens the understanding and confuses everyone by talking about these great mysteries of God in human ignorance? Job says, 'I am guilty. I have been talking all this time about things I did not understand. I have been speaking dogmatically and yet foolishly about things too wonderful for me. I thought I knew, but I didn't' (Rom. 11:33). Is not this the case today with the many religious voices heard in the land? Oh, that men would put their hands on their mouths (Job 40:4-5; Eccles. 5:1-2), until they have seen the Lord! Isaiah saw him and had something worthwhile to say (John 12:41).

'I have heard of thee by the hearing of the ear.' There are few in our land who cannot say, 'I have heard of thee by the hearing of the ear.'

1. God speaks in creation (Ps. 19:1-3).
2. God speaks in his law, written on heart and conscience (Rom. 2:14-15).
3. God speaks by his prophets and by that Prophet — his Son (Heb. 1:2).

4. God speaks through his written Word (John 20:31) so that all men are without excuse. Like Job, we can say that we have certainly heard of God.

'But now mine eye seeth thee.' This is not a vision, nor a dream, nor only an emotional spell. It is to see by faith the living God revealed in Christ Jesus our Lord. It is to understand something of the majesty and sovereignty of God. It is to understand something of the righteousness and holiness of God. It is to see him in his chief glory — his redemptive mercy and grace in Christ (Exod. 33:18-19).

1. *When did Job see the Lord?* When the Lord was pleased to reveal himself to Job (John 6:44-45; 1 Cor. 2:9-10). 'Flesh and blood did not reveal this to you, but my Father' (Matt. 16:17).

2. *What was Job's reaction when he saw the Lord?* He was filled with awe and reverence in the presence of the Lord. He put his hand on his mouth and stood in silence. He saw his evil nature in the only light in which it can be truly seen — the holiness of God. He confessed his sins and repented before God.

Questions

1. What is the difference between hearing about God and seeing him, by the eye of faith, as he really is?
2. You have heard about God. Have you seen him? What was your reaction?
3. What is the only valid response of a sinner before God?